Rags

The Autobiography of Derek Randall

Best Wishes

Derek Randall

Rags

The Autobiography of Derek Randall

with a Statistical Summary
by Peter Wynne-Thomas

Published by
SPORT-IN-PRINT, 3 RADCLIFFE ROAD, WEST BRIDGFORD,
NOTTINGHAM NG2 5FF

ISBN 0 947774 19 X

Photographic Acknowledgements:

John Sumpter	18, 31, 42, 146, 168, 173, 191, 194, 208, 215, 220, 225, 226
Patrick Eagar	11, 44, 188
T. Bailey Forman	34, 82, 198, 206, 216, 233
Geo. Herringshaw	56, 73, 154, 236
Retford Times	24
Newark Advertiser	48, 50, 143
T. Canham	64
Empics	66
S. Lindsell	71
S.L. Mehra	86
S. Pandit	94
Allsport	122, 156, 198, 222, 244
Ken Kelly	135
News Ltd., Sydney	162

Thanks to Mr. Brian Mather for his advice and assistance.

Typeset, printed and bound by Boots Print Ltd., Station Street, Nottingham NG2 3AA.

Contents

Preface

All of us, in our childhood, cherish extravagant ambitions. I am one of those fortunate few who managed to turn my boyish dreams into reality. Some may say it requires dedication amounting to ruthlessness to reach the very top in a particular occupation. I certainly wouldn't deny the need for dedication. In my case the dedication must be allied to the support and encouragement I received in my early days from my parents and my wife throughout virtually the whole of my career in county cricket.

I make no bones about the fact that I play cricket because I love the game and because of the enjoyment I get from it. I have always appreciated that the spectators, who come to cricket, pay my wages and I have therefore done my utmost to ensure that they have enjoyed watching the matches, in which I have been involved.

Cricket is a game that can be relished at many levels. Those of us who have made a full time career out of playing the game are grateful to the thousands who sit patiently watching our antics; in addition there are many more who follow cricket through television and radio. Judging by the number of books there are in the Trent Bridge library, there must also be thousands who enjoy reading about the game. They are the ones who will sit in judgement on this offering.

Readers who are in search of the caustic criticism and hints of scandal which seem to pepper some cricketers' autobiographies will find little to whet their appetites here, for this is the story of a happy cricketer, who has loved his days in county cricket and with very few exceptions, found that his efforts have been appreciated by cricket enthusiasts throughout the British Isles and in other parts of the world, Australia, New Zealand and the Indian sub-continent in particular.

May I close by thanking Peter Wynne-Thomas for his advice and providing the statistics, which have been cross-checked by Derek Drake and John and Michael Goulder, also Albert Bocking and Les Bullimore for suggesting this adventure into print. I am also grateful for permission to use the photographs which are reproduced, details are given in the acknowledgements.

Derek Randall
July 1992

CHAPTER 1

I make a start

There was little traffic as I crossed Gunthorpe Bridge and skirted past Caythorpe. It was one of those silly days between Christmas and the New Year, when English people don't quite know what to do. Liz had watched me fidgeting for most of the morning. She had found the kids something to occupy themselves. By lunchtime she'd made up her mind. "You may as well make a start today; if you hover about much longer, I'll throw something at you."

I pretended not to understand her, but it did me no good. "Go up to Retford and see your Mum and Dad: that's what Peter suggested, wasn't it?"

I negotiated the Lowdham roundabout and glanced at the little village cricket ground. I must have played a match or two there, but none sprang to mind. It had been a mild winter and even in late December, I think Ron Allsopp might have risked running the mower over the outfield.

How I'd been talked into writing a book, I don't quite know. One of my Benefit Committee had thrown up the idea at some meeting. I had given a very non-committal reply. I'm much happier with a bat and ball than with pen and paper. My spelling leaves something to be desired and at school, English grammar was a subject ideal for a dental appointment. Liz had got to hear of the idea and had said that I would probably have some time to spare during the winter months. Nothing had been said in the immediate rush up to Christmas. Rather foolishly, prompted by some book one of the children had been given, I mentioned the subject of my book and the reasons why I couldn't go ahead with it.

"You can borrow my dictaphone, Dad; only it'll probably need new batteries," said Simon helpfully. I find it a little irritating when my children solve difficulties I don't want solving.

"The tape runs about an hour and it's double-sided. You can talk into it and let a typist sort out the grammar and the spellings. Everyone does it like that these days."

I wasn't going to submit that easily. "You know what my memory's like. Trying to sort out the dates and the places and what happened in which match." I assumed my forlorn look. Megan doesn't like being left out of anything. She put in her twopennyworth: "There's those scrapbooks mum put in the bottom of the wardrobe in my room. I'll go and fetch them."

A dozen or so large scrapbooks were brought down and put on the dining room table. I began to look through them. Megan sat beside me.

"There's a nice photograph, Dad." It was the White Friars Hotel, somewhere in the depths of Sussex. Underneath, stuck on the same page, was the letter from Derrick Robins asking me to play for his team at Eastbourne in 1973 against the New Zealand touring team. My mother had cut out the newspaper reports and on the second day it was noted "Randall played a promising little innings". More significant was the report of the last day which showed: "Randall lbw b Hadlee 42." My first encounter with Richard Hadlee. There was no way of predicting then that he and I were to play against each other in many Tests, or indeed that for some ten years he would play for Notts.

Megan turned the pages. The main comments were reserved for the strange long hair styles of the early '70s.

I clutched at a straw. "There's nothing in these books about

Derrick Robin's Eleven at Eastbourne in 1973.

Notts winning the double. In fact there doesn't seem anything on the last ten years.''

Having got the dictaphone and the pile of scrapbooks, Liz was not going to be put off by some minor difficulty.

''There's that chap in the library at Trent Bridge. He's always telling you how many runs you need to break this record or that. I'll give the ground a ring and see if he's there.'' My wife had delivered the knockout punch.

Some days later, the scrapbooks were piled into the car; the dictaphone pushed into my pocket and I went down to the ground.

''Liz phoned you?''

A man in late middle-age with unruly grey hair looked up from his typewriter, the outline of which was just visible between mountains of books and a jungle of paper. The former all seem to have been opened at some important page and then discarded. The library looked as if it contained every volume ever written on cricket. Not only was every shelf full—and the shelves were a good eight feet high—but the large central table, the desk and most of the chairs also contained piles of books. I had known Peter Wynne-Thomas for ten or fifteen years and he seemed to have become part of the fabric of the pavilion, like my locker in the dressing room, or the Long Room bar.

He cleared two spaces. The first for me to sit down, the second for the scrapbooks.

''You're writing a book?''

I hesitated. ''Well, er. I wouldn't be quite as definite as that. The trouble is, I don't know where to start, and ...'' I might as well be honest. ''I don't know exactly what to put in it.'' I pulled the dictaphone out of my coat pocket.

''It's all very well Simon saying, 'Just chat into this machine'.''

Peter thumbled through the scrapbooks and began putting them into some sort of order.

''There's a tremendous lot on Test Cricket.''

''Yes, but it's rather been done to death; everybody's written about it. Mike Brearley's friend wrote a great description of one of my Test Hundreds. I'm sure I could use that again, if I asked him."

Peter went to a filing cabinet and pulled out a file.

"There's two books under your name already. One's a book mainly on coaching by Terry Bowles. The other's by that bod who writes for *The Times*, Alan Lee. It came out in 1984."

He got the two books down from the shelves. They looked familiar, I must have copies at home somewhere. I watched as he went fairly carefully through each book. The longer we sat in silence the more my hopes rose. A third book was clearly ridiculous.

"If the idea is to publish this book for 1993, then these two books give nothing on the last ten years, but what seems a little odd, there's very few pages on your early years."

The project was becoming serious again. I am someone, who, if I agree to do something, likes to do it to the best of my ability. It was at this point that I decided that I would go ahead with the book.

"Right, you tell me where to begin and I'll get on with it."

"I don't know if I'm the right person to ask, Derek, but from my personal viewpoint, like you, I was a very keen cricketer as a youngster, so what I, as a reader of your book, want to know is, what was it, in your young days that made you into an England Test player, whilst I never progressed beyond village cricket level. There's been dozens and dozens of books and newspaper articles on English Test cricket of the last twenty years; obviously you can put your view on it, but much of what you say is bound to be repetition. On the other hand no Test cricketer before has come from Retford, or anywhere within the Retford area. I suggest you go up to Retford and try and remember what the town was like twenty-five years ago. Talk to your Mum and Dad. Go to the cricket ground. Take your dictaphone and chat into it."

"Are you sure this is going to work?"

"Let's worry about that when you've filled your tape up."

I was now driving on the A614 passing Rufford Abbey and on the other side the new Center Parcs Sherwood Forest Holiday complex—Liz and I had taken the kids there for a long weekend—it had been great. Instead of going straight home—funny how I still call my parents' house home, though I've not lived there for twenty years—I drove through Ollerton and turned right at the Blue Tit. This road goes past the Bothamsall cricket ground. I played there, I can't remember exactly when, possibly for Retford Seconds or Jenkins. Dad was more familiar with it than I was. Dad used to play for NALGO whose team competed in the Retford & District League and the league was made up of village teams near Retford, such as Bothamsall, and various firms' sides from Retford itself. Dad bowled fast, but off the wrong foot. My first recollections of cricket are of playing in the garden at home with Mum and Dad. Mum bowled fast underarm. Then she'd have to go in, either to put the kettle on or sort out my younger brother or sister. Dad and I would play until it was too

A very early batting stance, the outfield's rather damp.

dark to see. I was England and he was Australia. One or two windows got broken in the process.

Dad would tell me of the first visit he ever made to Trent Bridge. He had been a member of the athletic team at Retford Grammar School and if the team won a particular match, the reward was a visit to watch England play Australia at Trent Bridge. Today with nearly everyone having a car, Trent Bridge seems no distance from Retford, but even when I was a youngster very few people went to Nottingham. The railway took you to Sheffield or Doncaster. It was to Doncaster I went when I studied as a mechanical draughtsman on a day release course from Jenkins. Although Retford is in Nottinghamshire, most visits were across the border into Yorkshire for major shopping items, or even watching League Football. So Dad's trip to the 1938 Test Match was a major event and something which he was fond of recalling.

The road had a flyover which crossed the A1. I was soon twisting through the little village of Gamston and joining the old Great North Road near the outskirts of Retford. It's amazing to think that when I first went to school, the Great North Road went through the middle of Retford and to get from my home on the Hallcroft Estate to school in Grove Street, I had to walk down Bridgegate and where Bridgegate joined the Market Square, a policeman was on permanent traffic duty, as the cars and lorries fought their way through the town centre.

I came to a sudden halt. Carolgate which took the Great North Road from the south into The Square had been closed to traffic, bricked over and pedestrianised (if such a word exists). I parked the car and walked. The Pheasant no longer existed. In the 1950s and 1960s it had been the headquarters of Retford cricket. Nowadays the pavilion at the cricket ground has a drinks licence, but then, after an evening's practice, the players would walk through the town to the Pheasant and sit in the little back room. Mr. Hall was the landlord. He was 'J.B.' to his contemporaries, but always Mr. Hall to the youngsters of my generation. Outside the building looked modest enough; built of brick, at a guess 150 years old. There were a few rooms upstairs for commercial travellers, but Mr. Hall lent an air of distinction to the establishment and for those in the know, it was regarded as one of the more superior pubs in the town. It was here that I crept in, no doubt under age, and had my first half of bitter. Mr. Hall would then have been in his 60s. He was a well built man something about six feet in height and convivial by nature. I'd never seen him play cricket, but I know he had played for Notts and gone overseas with Sir Julien Cahn's team. The way people spoke of Julien Cahn's team it seemed as if it was as important if not more so than the county side itself and everyone who had in any way a connection with Cahn seemed to have stories to tell about him. The thought of a millionaire running a first-class cricket team and taking it abroad each winter everywhere from New Zealand to South America sounds like some fairy tale, but Mr. Hall was living proof that Cahn's Team did exist. A good all-rounder, J.B. Hall had been brought up in Worksop, captained that side and then come to Retford, joined the local team and in 1949 led Retford to the Bassetlaw League Championship. The first time the town club had won the title.

Whilst J.B. Hall was the father figure of Retford cricket, when I was a youth his son was the driving force behind the current First Eleven. Michael Hall, a few inches taller than his father, but with similar features, had been the leading cricketer at Retford Grammar School and had just got into the Retford First Eleven the year his father took the club to the title. Mike had been on the staff at Trent Bridge through most of the 1950s and was a very talented right hand batsman. He spent every evening down at the cricket ground organising fielding practice or net practice and he was an inspiration to all the young players.

I stood in the middle of Carolgate. The cinema had gone, but one shop which still remained more or less unchanged was Retford Sports. It was here that I bought much of my cricket equipment—I seem to remember my first purchase was a pair of batting gloves. There'd been a small fete in the playing fields next to the Hallcroft Estate and I had paid sixpence to plunge a stick into a sandpit on the buried treasure stall. I'd won first prize. I don't remember how much, but it was enough to buy batting gloves.

Some hundred and fifty yards away Carolgate opened up into The Square, where the market was held once or twice a week. The Square was another piece of the new pedestrianisation. There was the war memorial in the centre but dominating the place was the rather florid Town Hall. For hundreds of years Retford had been a small agricultural market town, but, whenever they built the railways, it had suddenly become a major railway junction—as it still is—I suppose the money from the railway was enough to let the Town Council build a grand Town Hall.

As an international cricketer I seem to have attended almost as many 'grand banquets' as I've made runs, but rather like my batting gloves, it was the first such affair which I recall with most pleasure. Retford won the Bassetlaw League title in both 1968 and 1969 and in the latter year held, what the menu—another memento my mother stuck in the scrapbook—described as the 'Bassetlaw League Championship Dinner' in the Town Hall. Mike Hall gave a detailed account of the team's performance during the year. Harold Rhodes the England and Derbyshire fast bowler spoke of his cricket career, but I was more impressed by the brief speech of Rupert Spencer, a leading Retford businessman and partner in the auctioneers, Henry Spencer and Son. He praised cricket in general and Retford cricket in particular, but I suppose it was the way he put over his speech that held the attention—especially of an eighteen year old who can't keep still!

Being unable to keep still brings to mind an incident that occurred either during that summer or the one which followed. John Cook was a few years older than me, but like me he used to go down to the Retford ground for practice every evening. We lived two or three streets from each other. John had joined the police force on leaving school and because he worked shifts had

John Cook, who had to use his handcuffs.

problems playing in some matches. In the match in question at Retford he must have been on evening shift, so arrived for the afternoon game complete with uniform so that he could go straight from the ground to the station. It was a vital game and I was getting more and more excited over the result. The rest of the players, including John, got increasingly fed up as I jumped up and down. In the end John couldn't stand it any more. He grabbed me—he is a strong tall man—and dragged me to the Gents. Whipping his handcuffs out of his pocket, he handcuffed me to the lavatory cistern and went back to watch the finish of the match. I was released when it was time to go home.

Apart from my fidgeting, another habit of mine which some players didn't take too kindly to was my attitude at the end of a hard day's play. The players changed and it was off to the pub for a pint. I didn't drink, but even those who were not keen on beer would go for the hospitality and probably have a shandy. Not me. As soon as the game finished I wanted to go into the nets for an hour or, if I could find no one to bowl at me, I would practice fielding, picking up the ball and throwing it at a single stump. I didn't want to leave the cricket field.

I wandered back down Carolgate and picked up the car. A new road now diverted traffic round the back of New Street. The tumbledown old buildings that used to be Oates Builders Merchants had gone. The new road went behind the church avoiding the cannon, a relic of some war, was it the Crimean? Eventually I came to the roundabout off which there were six roads, the most important of which was Cricket Field Lane.

Cricket Field Lane was a dead end, which led only to the Retford Cricket Club ground and a few modern bungalows. I walked through the gate beside the new brick pavilion. Dictaphone in hand, I checked to see if the little lights came on when you pressed the button and then thought about something to say.

The cricket ground has changed a great deal in the thirty or more years since I first walked through the fields near my home and entered it, via the gap in the thorn hedge. Mum claims she took me to the ground in my pram: that may well be so, but my memory won't stretch back that far. I must have been seven or eight when I first 'discovered' the ground for myself and within two years I was spending every summer evening there. Mum and Dad were very concerned when I didn't come home till ten at night and I know Mum checked with John Cook, who was five years my senior, to make certain I was at the cricket ground and not wandering round Retford. I found I had a tremendous ball sense and even as a youngster, no fear of the hardness of a cricket ball. Mike Hall would hit the ball high in the air right across the ground for fielding practice and for a lark I would nip round and try to catch the ball before the official member of the First Eleven could reach it.

When I first remember the ground there were tennis courts and a bowling green, though the latter was overgrown. The ground was also famous for its slope, which batsmen always turned to take advantage of—that was on the west side and at the foot of the slope were tall trees and a ditch. About the age of fourteen or fifteen the infamous slope (the ground has since been levelled) was nearly the end of my cricketing career. I was driving the club's roller, going carefully backwards and forwards over the outfield when my shoe caught under the brake pedal just as the roller began descending the slope. As it gathered speed I desperately struggled to regain control and only managed to do so just before the roller toppled into the ditch.

The old wooden pavilion has been replaced by a smart brick building and overlooking the ground on two sides are modern bungalows. The dirt track, in the wide thick undergrowth of whose verges many a young cricketer dallied with his sweetheart, and I was no exception, has been tarmaced and no longer contains secrets.

I tried to visualise the evenings when I came in the hope of

The Retford Eleven under J. B. Hall – The old pavilion in the background.

being given a turn in the nets or fielding practice. The real diehard regulars were Mike Hall himself, Alan Bull, Tony Smith, John Brown and John Cook; others came and went. After it became too dark to see the cricket, I recall Mike Hall and Tony Smith positioning their cars with lights on to form two goal posts; the football came out and we played a knockabout game for another half hour or so. John Brown was a very useful bowler who later moved to Steetley. Alan Bull was an off spinner who got a lot of turn on the ball and a much better batsman than he admitted. I recall one occasion when Mike Hendrick was pro-ing for Glapwell and Bull simply hit him all over the ground. Alan had been on the staff at Trent Bridge for a season or two and had acted as substitute fielder in a Test.

The dictaphone was still in my hand, but I wondered how much of this was worth recording. I glanced at my watch. Mum and Dad would have tea on the table, I'd better go.

CHAPTER 2

At Home

"That you, Derek?" Mum's voice from the living room as I came through the door.

"Sorry I'm late, I stopped off at the ground."

"Liz mentioned something about a book." Dad switched off the sound on the telly. Mum got up and went in the dining room to finish setting the table.

"I just want a few stories about cricket when I lived in Retford, before I got into the county team."

"You mean like when you used to get up at the crack of dawn and hitch a lift in Clark's laundry van from whatsisname who lived in Hallcroft Road? They've closed down, you'd never have thought it. One of the best known businesses in Retford. West Retford Hall, where the Clarks lived, is a restaurant, you know."

"Wait a minute Dad, I haven't switched the dictaphone on. Anyway, do you think people are interested in me travelling from home to Trent Bridge with the clean linen?"

"I know what you mean, you want more on the actual cricketing side. I think you ought to mention your uncle Derek—you were named after him. He made quite a name for himself in local cricket."

Grandma Amy and my mum.

Mum joined in, "Didn't Bill take six wickets with six balls for Moorgate United?"

"He did, and then when I mentioned it some years later, no one remembered it. But I'm sure it happened; it was on the British Rail ground under Babworth Bridge. Even Bill himself didn't remember." (Bill was Mum's brother.)

"We haven't heard what the children got for Christmas. Is the family coming up at the weekend?"

Things didn't seem to be going quite according to plan.

"Tea'll be ready in a minute, Derek. D'you want ice cream or custard on the fruit, only I think I'm out of custard powder." Dad got up and went into the dining room. I switched the dictaphone off.

"D'you remember all the fuss you caused when you lost that precious bat at Cleethorpes? Grandma Amy bought it for you when we went there for the summer holidays. You wouldn't be parted from it. Even brought it with you to breakfast. Then we were walking along the main shopping street and suddenly you realised you weren't carrying your bat. The world had come to an end. Grandma retraced our steps, going into all the shops we'd visited and she found it leaning against a counter in a sweet shop."

I laughed. I'm forever mislaying things now, they turn up again, but that bat. It was one of those cheap kid's bats, very pale looking, made in Pakistan or India. There was a knot in the middle of the blade which kept coming out. I wonder what happened to that bat. Dad and I used it when we played cricket in the back garden. I looked out of the dining room window. The stretch of grass which had formed our pitch now had a flower bed in the middle of it. Dad wasn't much of a gardener and I'd come up at sometime and dug up a patch, planting some flowers. I wonder what did happen to my very first bat?

"When you were about eleven or twelve you used to go down to the ground with your bag for every match, hoping that someone'd fail to turn up and you'd be pushed in as eleventh man, or failing that field as substitute."

Mum smiled, but I thought of that match at Manton. Somehow I had got the last place in the Retford Second Eleven team. Les Beevers was the Retford captain. Manton scored about 140 and Retford were 60 for nine when I went in to partner Les. The bar was open and at the sight of me, a small twelve year old, arriving at the wicket as last man, the fielders could already taste the pint they'd be drinking in a minute or two. I had other ideas and at about quarter past eight, the umpires declared the match drawn due to bad light. The score was 92 for nine. I don't think I was too popular that night.

The following season I almost hit the headlines as a bowler. A crumpled cutting saved by Mum described a Sunday match against Ruston Bucyrus and one paragraph runs:

'The visitors, owing to a transport mix-up, had arrived at West Retford minus their opening bowler and Retford's brightest hope for the future, 13 year old Derek Randall, substituted for him. As a reward for a splendid little effort with the bat and even more splendid efforts in the field, the visiting skipper offered him the ball when defeat for his side was a mere formality. Young Randall grasped the opportunity by bowling admirably and induced Newman to edge a catch to keeper Daley off a forward defensive stroke. Later he also passed Hall outside the off stump before the home skipper hit Enderby straight for the winning runs to bring Retford home to an eight wicket victory. It must be a long time since a 13 year old lad led the players off the field at West Retford and deservedly so too!'

My cricket equipment at this time still comprised a pair of plimsolls and my batting gloves which I brought in a carrier bag. Otherwise I used the stuff from the club bag. Due to a bit of good fortune which came Dad's way, I did eventually get a proper bat of my own. Dad worked part time for Freddie Acres, a bookmaker in Retford, and one weekend picked up an unexpected bonus. He took me round to the sports shops in Carolgate and I chose my first bat.

There'd been no cricket at my Primary School in Grove

Street and at the Milner School, I doubt if I played more than six or seven games all the time I was there. Football was more popular. I had been quite keen on football. Roger Turner had been my great footballing friend. He'd played in the school team on the right wing and I'd been inside right. We become known as 'tip and tap', being good at running with the ball and passing between us but I didn't have the power to drive the ball hard. I was forever kicking pebbles along the pavement and getting into trouble for wearing out the toes of my shoes.

"D'you remember, Dad, taking me down to Trent Bridge for coaching in the nets?"

He shook his head. "There was the time you went by train to Cleethorpes to represent Notts against Lincolnshire. Was it Under 16s? Your mother wasn't at all happy with you going by yourself, but you insisted and we gave way."

I must have grown up a bit by then. The memory I had was of going by bus with my parents to Trent Bridge. They handed me

On holiday in Cleethorpes with my brother and sister, the year I had my first bat.

over to John Clay and went off to shop in the city centre. I'd never been to Nottingham before. I had a marvellous afternoon in the nets. When the session ended I packed up my bag, the other boys went their various ways and soon I was standing in the entrance to the ground alone. I felt utterly lost as time passed and there was no sign of Mum and Dad. By the time they actually arrived I was close to tears. I felt as if I'd been abandoned miles from home and I hadn't the slightest idea how to get back to Retford.

Looking back with the knowledge I now have of club cricket in Nottinghamshire, I was very fortunate that, not only were my parents and my uncles very keen on cricket and did all they could to encourage me, but also I lived virtually within a stone's throw of the best run and strongest Cricket Club in the county. I had my first trial in Notts Second Eleven in 1969 and the regular First Team of Retford in that season contained no less than nine players who had represented Notts at Second Eleven level, three of whom had been professionals on the Trent Bridge staff. So the professionalism and competitive spirit in the Retford side in the late '60s transmitted itself to the young players in the Club. I may be doing one or two of the other teams in the county a disservice, but there was no denying that the Bassetlaw League was the strongest League and that Retford were the Champions in both 1968 and 1969, so the results really speak for themselves. On the other hand there was a great divide between the cricket clubs in the north of the county, the best of whom played in the Bassetlaw League and the Nottingham-based Notts Cricket Association. Clubs such as Retford, Worksop, Steetley were not members of the Association.

"Derek, have you mentioned Frank Woodhead or Jack Elliott; both of them helped you a lot."

I switched on the dictaphone, trying to collect my thoughts on both Frank Woodhead and Jack Elliott. Frank's mission in life—at least in the 1960s and 70s when I got to know him—was to build up a Notts cricket team made up of Notts-born cricketers. He had played for the county in the days of Larwood and Voce when the rule was that Notts only played cricketers born in the county. The club had abandoned that rule in the early 1950s, by which time Frank had retired as a professional and combined his job as a solicitor's clerk with coaching at Nottingham High School. By the 1960s there was scarcely a Nottingham born cricketer playing in the county eleven and it was then that Frank started his campaign. Although over fifty he more or less appointed himself captain of the Notts Colts Team which was set up in 1962 and running that side scoured the county for new players to represent the Colts. Frank couldn't do enough for any young player and I know that Bruce French, Kevin Cooper and all the others who were recruited through his 'system' on to the Trent Bridge playing staff in the 1970s will agree with me, when I say that we owe much to Frank Woodhead. In 1970 he appointed himself county coach and remained in that post for ten years before retiring. Jack Elliott was one of the mainstays of the Notts Cricket Association. I remember staying the night at his house in West Bridgford when I played at Trent Bridge, because of the difficulty of travelling back to Retford. At the time I first met him he was Chairman of the Notts Youth Cricket Council, but I think he must have been on every committee connected with cricket in Nottinghamshire. He was elected President of the County Cricket Club in February 1980, but died suddenly within a month of taking up office.

Going back to the Retford side of the 1960s, I should mention one or two of the other players. Geoff Key was on the staff at Trent Bridge for a couple of years, he was a very, very good player, but he lacked the physical strength to develop into a county cricketer; he's a hairdresser in Retford. John Coddington, a medium-fast bowler, I never saw bowl a bad ball. He died a couple of years ago in an accident at the pit. He was the sort of person for whom I never heard anyone have a bad word. Derek Armstrong was one of the leading batsmen in the side, but later he seemed to suffer from nerves and after a bad run of scores finished playing. Colin Loates was a local farmer, also involved in the sale of agricultural equipment; he was one of the work horses of the club. Freddie Self was a school teacher at Ranby Prep School. He played in various trials whilst at Cambridge, but didn't get a blue. Freddie captained Retford before Mike Hall and was the team's wicketkeeper, always immaculate. He was also the most stylish batsman in the team. Keith Jackson was an out and out Yorkshireman. He played a few games for Yorkshire Seconds as a left arm quick bowler—he also played odd matches for Notts Seconds, but the family were fanatical Tykes. He later went to play for British Ropes—originally Ordsall Wire Works, now Bridon. The standard of that side's cricket was to grow to rival Retford in more recent times. To the outsider, Ordsall is part of Retford, but once it was a separate village centred round a church about a mile or so south of Retford's market square.

Jim Harkin was a stylish left hand batsman, who bowled right arm off spinners. Jim went to Maltby Grammar School, as did the Loates—Colin and his brother John. John Loates had played for Retford as a schoolboy, but moved to Steetley and Jim Harkin left Retford to join John Loates at that club. Both were mainstays of the Bassetlaw League and of Steetley for the best part of twenty years. John Cook, the off spinner, had left Retford in 1965, due to living in Mansfield, but returned to the club in 1970—he was later to play for Notts (the second Retford born Notts first-class cricketer, after myself). I know I've already said it before, but I can't emphasise too strongly the role of Mike Hall. At the time of which I'm now talking, the end of the '60s, he had played about twenty years for Retford; it wouldn't be too much to say that we looked up to him as a god.

"I was just thinking about Mike Hall, Dad."

"I don't know whether I ever mentioned this before. I remember coming home from Jenkins one evening (Dad was the chief estimator there) and stopping at the cricket ground just to see what was going on. You were batting in the nets and Mike Hall was coaching you. Suddenly he snapped out, 'If you back away once more, you'll be out the team for Saturday.' His tone was such that I felt like telling him that if he was going to take that

Bob White, the gnarled professional trained at Lord's.

Mike Hall, who installed his enthusiasm into the young cricketers of Retford.

attitude, then my son would go and play for another club. I didn't, I thought, he knows best how to improve your batting.''

Dad was right, but there was one habit which Mike Hall drilled in to me that I find hard to break, but is not popular. He said never walk unless the umpire gives you out.

By 1969 I had set my heart on a career in cricket; I was 18 and had been working at Jenkins for three years. Jenkins was an engineering firm in Thrumpton Lane, just before you got to the level crossing and off the Great North Road as you approached Retford from the south. They mainly made machinery for the coal industry. I went straight there from school and like all the apprentices I went from one department to another, learning the various aspects of the production. I ended in the drawing office and later studied HNC mechanical engineering draughtsmanship. Mike Hall, knowing my keenness to become a professional cricketer, was aware that most of the players who get on to a county staff either fail after a year or two, or what is probably worse survive for seven or eight years and then have to find another job in their late twenties. If you have no qualifications you can then be in a serious situation, perhaps with a young family and no income. Mike hammered home to me the need to get some paper qualifications so that I had something to fall back on. I was young and foolish, I ignored the advice. I went to Doncaster Technical College, but never bothered to take the exams. I was lucky that Jenkins were very kind to me and employed me during the winter for the first few years I was on the staff at Trent Bridge. I feel I ought to have done more to repay their kindness, but my head was full of cricket and very little else interested me.

''What year was it that I played for Notts Seconds, Dad?''

''It was mid week, you had to have three days off work and I'm sure it was played at Steetley.''

''I think Jim Harkin played—perhaps I went there with Jim? I've got it. We were playing Derbyshire. Mike Hendrick opened their bowling, but the bowler who baffled me was the slow left-armer, Freddie Swarbrook. I don't think either Jim or myself made double figures in either innings. That was the same year I arranged my summer holidays to suit the Notts Youth matches. Sometime in August, there were about ten one day matches one after the other. I had one day of success, scoring eighty odd at Cambridge. I remember rushing round trying to find a phone, so I could let you know how I'd got on."

"Have a look in that scrapbook when you get back to Nottingham, Derek."

Mum came in from doing the washing up. "You've mentioned Freddie Stinchcombe. He played for Notts didn't he? He certainly spent hours bowling at you in the nets ... and Tim Jones, he played for Notts Seconds."

"Mum, I'm not sure that people will be all that interested. What about some photographs?"

"I'll go and get the box."

"Let me go."

"No Derek, I know exactly where they are, you'll only start rummaging about."

I began going through the tin biscuit box, which was the family album. There was the picture of Dad in his naval uniform, various holiday snaps and more formal pictures of wedding groups.

"Where are the cricket pictures, Mum?"

"You might well ask. How many times have you been here and said, can I borrow this photo, Mum, can I borrow that one. Do we ever see them again? It's the same with your medals and things, if I hadn't kept those one or two in the china cabinet, we'd have nothing."

Mother wasn't too pleased. It was a sore point. I looked at my watch. It was time I was going. I'd told Liz I'd be back by seven. There was a bit of a frost outside and I wanted to be gone before the roads became icy. That steep hill by the Farnsfield roundabout could be dodgy.

I suppose I'd got somewhere. One way or another I'd filled up one side of the tape. The difficulty is that I'm basically a shy

Dad, Liz, myself and mum after I returned from Australia in 1977.

person, I prefer to be at home rather than propping up a bar swopping stories. Even when I'm on tour I like to be in bed early. Ten o'clock's quite late enough for me. I'm not a great one for the cricketer's version of fisherman's yarns, like Freddie Trueman. The stories are good for a laugh, but most of them don't ring true: not that I can remember them anyway. At the other extreme there are those who spend hour after hour discussing the technicalities of the game. I recalled the solitary hours I'd spent rolling a ball along the ground, running after it, picking it up, turning round and throwing it at a single stump. Doing it again and again until I hit the stump more often than not. It was a question of practice and more practice. Reading about it in a book, but discussing it in the bar wasn't much help really. But when it comes to writing a book, it takes a sentence to say that, whereas a funny story can fill a page or two.

Some on-coming headlights temporarily blinded me. ''Idiot.'' Then I remembered I forgot to dip mine. I went over Gunthorpe Bridge and climbed the hill past East Bridgford. Bob

White lived there. What was that crack Ken Taylor'd come out with? It was when we won the Championship in 1981 and there was a dinner. Ken was commenting on how well off professionals were compared with his day. He'd pointed at Bob, who'd just retired from first-class cricket. "There's Bob, a gnarled old pro from London, and now he's living in the stockbroker belt of Nottingham." Well, Bob had worked hard for what he had.

I left the main road and was soon parking the car in the drive. Just about an hour, door to door. Odd that, it didn't seem to matter whether it was night or day, rush hour, or empty road, the journey always took an hour, give or take five minutes.

Liz had her feet up on the couch watching some play on telly.

"Kids in?"

"They've just gone up the road to see a friend. How did it go?"

"I'll play the tape."

I fiddled with the various switches and buttons. Silence. Liz had a go. Still silence.

"That's wasted an afternoon."

Simon and Megan returned. Simon looked at it, made a few adjustments. Suddenly: sound.

"You have to rewind it, Dad." He gave me his withering look.

The four of us sat round the dining table listening to the conversations of my parents and myself. After about quarter of an hour, Simon and Megan wandered off. Some minutes later, Liz spoke.

"It's a bit of a muddle. You're sure people are going to be interested in all that stuff about Retford and those lads you played football with and Mr. Hall's pub."

"Peter suggested it."

"You'd better go and see him. Play him the tape. That'll change his mind."

A couple of days later I had to go to Trent Bridge to see

Gary Sobers batting, Mike Smedley at the other end.

Sheila (that's Sheila Ball, the physio) about a problem with my foot. I called in at the library.

''Sorry, it won't work.''

''This is interesting.'' Peter looked up from another mountain of paper. ''In 1992, you'll have been a capped player for Notts for twenty seasons—right?''

''Yes, that's right.''

''The system of awarding county caps on an official basis started about 1921. There's not a single player who's actually survived twenty years as a capped player until now, if you chop the six wartime years from Hardstaff, Keeton and so on. That must be worth a line somewhere in the book, mustn't it?''

I must have looked a bit down in the mouth.

''If you're not interested...''

''It's not that, I've been to Retford to see Mum and Dad, but Liz reckons what I brought back on the tape's rubbish. I think they said 200 pages, I can't even get the first half dozen right.''

''Let's pretend you're batting. You've played and missed most of the balls in the first over. You don't say to Chris Broad, I'm going home now. You concentrate, get the pace of the wicket and before you know where you are, a four or two have come and you're as happy as a sandboy.''

I was still very dubious.

''Tell you what. Leave the tape, I'll play it back and type out what's on it. It can't be as grim as you think; you're too pessimistic!''

The phone rang. It was for me.

''I've got to go up to Worksop. If Harold comes looking for me, can you apologize for me? I was going to spend an hour in the nets with him.'' The problem of being a 40 year old county cricketer is that half your mind is on the future. The phone call had been from Liz regarding a meeting with a possible business contact. It was not something I could afford to ignore.

It must have been a week or so later, when I went to the library again. It was filled with some visitors being given a tour of the cricket ground. I signed some autograph books as Harry Dalling took them off to inspect the Long Room.

"Sorry I've not been back before, you know what it's like."

"I don't think it's quite as hopeless as you believed, Derek. What I've done is a statistical survey of your career to date."

Peter handed me a wad of paper.

"Use that as an appendix at the back of the book. It should keep the statistical nuts happy. Can I make another suggestion?"

I was happy to accept any idea. Two or three weeks had gone without any real progress. On April 1st, John Birch demanded that we report back for fulltime pre-season training.

"Anything," I said.

"Pick up a dozen matches which you particularly remember and tell the story of the game, the people who played in it and perhaps, what actually happened before it."

So that is how this book evolved. I made up my list; had frequent visits to the library, digging out press cuttings and scorebooks. Gradually the book took shape.

CHAPTER 3

Six into the Cemetery

"When's the season starting, Fred?"

"If you've asked me that once, you've asked a dozen times. Anyhow, why the sudden interest in cricket? You're not thinking of turning out for the works team, are you?"

'It's nothing to do with work's side, Fred; it's your lad. If he uses up any more tracing paper trying to draw that new spindle, there won't be any forests left in Brazil. He makes more use of his Tee-square practising cover drives than drawing straight lines."

"He reports back to Trent Bridge at the beginning of April."

"He might have finished that spindle by then, but if it turns out the right size it'll be a miracle. I think I'll set him on drawing cricket balls next winter."

Happily I was in blissful ignorance of this conversation between the head draughtsman David Harrison and Dad. It was a little story he would relate with relish in later years.

After one match for Notts Second in 1969, I had played half a dozen or so games either in the Second Eleven Competition or for Notts Club & Ground during 1970 and scored enough runs to be offered a place on the playing staff in 1971. Since it wasn't practical to travel by public transport on a daily basis from Retford to Trent Bridge, the club had found me a room at the YMCA in

The Notts first team when I joined the Trent Bridge staff.

Shakespeare Street—opposite the Victoria Centre. Not being the kind of person who makes friends at the drop of a hat, I found life in the YMCA very lonely. I was happy enough at the cricket ground, but didn't look forward to the evenings spent in the hostel.

Dad solved the problem for 1972, finding me a room with Mrs. Perkins, a friend of a friend, who lived out not far from Trent Bridge, in West Bridgford. So for my second season as a professional cricketer, I left Retford for the very homely surroundings of Mrs. Perkins house in Byron Road—I was much happier.

I had only been given a contract for one year. To me this meant that if I didn't obtain a place in the First Eleven during 1972, I faced the prospect of my career in county cricket finishing almost before it had begun: I had appeared in one First Team match in 1971, that was the Sunday League game at the Player's Ground against Surrey. I didn't bat and we lost. Financial problems meant that the County Club had to be fairly ruthless in its hiring and firing of players. Alan Bull and Geoff Key, two of the best players Retford had produced had got on to the Trent Bridge staff, but never played in the First Team; Mike Hall had been a little more fortunate, but never commanded a regular First Team place.

Mentally I went through my innings with the Seconds in 1971. I hadn't scored a hundred. My average in the mid twenties placed me between Peter Plummer, who was chiefly played for his bowling, and Dusty Hare. All three of us were well below Peter Johnson, Jack Frost, Nirmal Nanan and skipper Bill Russell. It was not going to be easy.

Cricket's a team game, however only eleven players can be fitted into any one side. Since I had no bowling ability—I did take a wicket with my first ball in Second Eleven cricket, but no one takes my bowling too seriously—I had to occupy one of the six batting places in the county side. In 1971 the first five in the line-up had been Harris, Bolus, Hassan, Smedley and Sobers. 'Pasty'

Graham Frost, a friendly rival for a batting place.

Brian Bolus, Notts captain in my first match for the county.

Harris had had a record breaking summer in 1971, topping 2,000 runs and averaging above fifty. At 28 he was an extremely competent opening batsman, just below international level, with probably ten more summers in front of him. He had spent the winter playing for Eastern Province and coaching in South Africa. He had returned looking sun tanned and very fit. Brian Bolus, the Yorkshireman with a persuasive turn of phrase, had begun as an attacking batsman, but was now more defensive than Harris and ten years his senior. He'd played a few Tests for England some years before and still had several seasons of county cricket left in him.

The enthusiastic 'Basher' Hassan had come from Nairobi to qualify for Notts. For a year or two he had had a problem being an overseas player and therefore had not always managed to keep a place in the team. A couple of seasons back he had become a regular First Team man and his awkward stance was now a well-known feature of the county circuit, as was his brilliant fielding at bat-pad.

Mike Smedley, a quiet batsman with strokes full of style, had batted very well in 1971 and made over 1,500 runs. He was the dependable type of cricketer who formed the backbone of county cricket.

The fifth batsman on my list was simply the world's greatest cricketer. Gary Sobers treated county bowling with disdain. It was a pity for Notts that by the time he joined the county his best years were behind him, but he was still a magnificent player to watch. He had missed many county games due to injury or Test calls, but everyone hoped that he would be able to play throughout 1972.

I have gone into the composition of the side in some detail in order to give an idea what Bruce French might term, the Everest I had to climb. Bruce has had a go at persuading me to climb mountains, but I have never taken to the sport.

The summary of the above meant that barring accidents five batting places for the 1972 season were filled. In 1971 the sixth batting place had been shared between Jack Frost and Richard

Basher Hassan, the fearless fielder at bat-pad and determined run-getter.

Bielby, with Frost getting preference towards the end of the summer. Richard had left the staff and therefore the competition for the final batting place was between Jack Frost, Nirmal Nanan, Paul Todd, Dusty Hare and myself.

Put down on paper, this all reads rather clinical and unfriendly, but if I wanted to earn a living as a county cricketer, I certainly wasn't going to achieve that ambition playing for the Seconds.

Graham 'Jack' Frost was a local Nottingham batsman, who had been playing, on and off, for five years in the First Team. His career had reached a crucial stage. Dusty Hare from a farming family near Newark had joined the Trent Bridge staff with me. He was a talented rugger player and it was already becoming clear that he would soon have to choose between the two sports at top class level. Nirmal Nanan came from Trinidad. He had settled in Nottingham with the object of becoming qualified for England by residence. Paul Todd was two years younger than me. He had scored a vast amount of runs in Nottingham club cricket in 1971 and had joined the staff at the beginning of the season.

Having given details of the batsmen at Trent Bridge for 1972, it might be appropriate to remind the reader of the overall county scene in that year. The Gillette Cup had been going since 1963 and the Sunday League, sponsored by John Player, since 1969. For the coming year a third competition, the Benson & Hedges Cup, had been added and the traditional County Championship fixture list had been reduced from 24 to 20 matches to fit the B&H in. Whether this was a good or bad move was not for me to say, but more One Day matches meant that more importance would be placed on fielding, saving runs being even more vital than taking wickets. The hours and hours I'd spent in fielding practice at Retford seemed to be time well-spent.

As the batsman in possession, Jack Frost was given the sixth batting place—not necessarily batting at no.6—for the first games of the new season. Brian Bolus chose to move down the batting order. During the last few years he and Mike Harris had been

Notts regular opening pair, but he went in no.4 and Frost opened with Harris.

Just as the season started Sobers announced that he wished to be relieved of the captaincy and vice-captain Bolus was given the post. After half a dozen games, during which Frost failed to reach fifty, he was dropped and Nirmal Nanan promoted. Bob White who in recent times had batted at no.7 or even 8 was moved up to open the innings with Harris and the young West Indian went in at seven.

Since I spent the early part of 1972 either playing with Notts Second or the Club & Ground and on Saturdays turning out for Retford, most of the detailed information on Notts First Team performances came secondhand. Our results were not very brilliant, we had failed to win any of the first five first-class games, had lost two out of three Sunday matches, but won two out of three Benson & Hedges games.

On Tuesday May 30, the three day Championship game with Leicestershire at Trent Bridge ended in disaster. Our batting failed twice. Graham McKenzie and Ken Higgs dismissed us for 143 and 137—Raymond Illingworth, the Leicester captain, didn't even bother to bowl a single over himself. Leicestershire were one of the best sides in the Championship that year, but the wickets at home were not as green as they later became.

The game finished early and Brian Bolus told me that I would be included in the side to play Essex at Newark the following day. As it was just as easy to travel from Retford to Newark compared with going from West Bridgford. I went back to Retford that night. My grandparents would be anxious not to miss the game and therefore would take me by car to the ground for the start of play.

I went to bed early. Not that that is anything new. I prefer to be in bed by 10 o'clock, much to the annoyance of some of my room mates on tour, who seem to be able to stay up half the night and still be fit to play the next day. As soon as it was light I was downstairs, making a cup of coffee and by the time the car was packed, I had been twitching to be off for several hours. The journey and my arrival at the ground went by as a blur and is now totally forgotten. We must have gone over the bridge and past the castle—like Retford, Newark is another town through which the Great North Road no longer passes. The ground is down a dead end off what used to be the A1. It had been built as the sports ground for Ransome and Marles, a ball-bearing firm. There was a football ground on the left hand side with a stand and beyond the cricket square, tennis courts and a bowling green. The pavilion was a modest single storey timber building and alongside was a social club. It was very much the same as many of the better clubs in the Bassetlaw League.

Almost every player must suffer from nerves on his debut and when his debut is at Trent Bridge or one of the other top grounds then it is difficult not to be overawed by the surroundings. I still didn't regard Trent Bridge as my cricketing home because the county Second Eleven very rarely played there. Despite having represented Notts in many matches just below first-class standard, I doubt if I'd appeared in a game at Trent Bridge more than two or three times in four years.

I was lucky therefore that my debut match was to be played in familiar surroundings. I might be somewhat overawed by the company I was keeping, but not by the venue.

There had been rain overnight. The start was delayed. Sitting around looking at the bits of blue sky between the clouds did nothing to calm my nerves. The other players, used to the accommodation in the pavilion at Trent Bridge, were wandering around almost as if it had been an away game. Notts usually only played one game a year at Newark and even that had only been arranged during the last few seasons. We had lunch and about the middle of the afternoon the game started. Our opponents, Essex, won the toss and decided to bat. I was not unhappy at the decision. Our seam bowlers, Barry Stead and Bill Taylor made the ball move off the seam and shoot through. I didn't envy the batsmen one bit.

Barry Stead was what I regard as a typical Yorkshire type. Of medium height with fair hair somewhat thinning he came from somewhere on the outskirts of Leeds and had been at Trent Bridge about ten years. He bowled left arm pretty brisk and came in to wave his bat near the bottom of the order. One of those people who continually muddle up their words, I was never quite sure if this was deliberate or not.

If he wanted you to go into the nets for practice, he would comment: "I've asked you here to insist me." Later in 1972 I went to London with the Notts team for the first time. We were playing Surrey at The Oval and had some time to kill. Barry said he would show me the sights. We drove past numerous statues, all of which Barry pointed out with the comment:

"That's a nice ornament."

Eventually we landed up in Trafalgar Square. It was becoming very clear that Barry's knowledge of London was a trifle limited. Barry pointed up at Nelson's column:

The Notts team coming on to the field at Newark. I seem to be last!

"That's another nice ornament."

At the time our wicketkeeper was the cheerful Dave Pullan, another Yorkshireman. Much banter and obscure Yorkshire jokes passed between the two during the course of a day's cricket. Dave lost his place in the Notts side when the policy was changed and a batsman who could keep wicket was preferred to a specialist behind the stumps. Myself, I am happier if the best wicketkeeper available is picked. A dropped catch or missed stumping can depress a side more quickly than the fact that the total is twenty runs less.

Essex muddled through to reach 119 all out. Like most people when Essex is mentioned, I nowadays think of the best or one of the best teams in the country. Twenty years ago Essex had never won a trophy and never looked like winning anything. They were one of the 'also rans' of county cricket.

For Notts to bowl out Essex for a small score was not, in 1972, the feat it would have been ten years later with the likes of Gooch and McEwan in the side. The Essex bowling however was beginning to show the signs of strength which caused havoc a few years afterwards. I sat tight lipped as in gloomy light Mike Harris and Bob White went in to bat. Both were professionals of what I termed the 'old school', they had been trained at Lord's before moving to Trent Bridge. Harris had a very sound technique and was powerful off the front foot. White, dark haired with a slightly ruddy complexion, batted left handed. At Lord's he'd scarcely ever bowled, but with Notts he soon became the main off spinner in the side.

Harris played back to the second ball of the innings, Boyce, the talented West Indian, made it shoot through and Harris was judged leg before. Bolus sent in Dave Pullan. He managed a push which he scampered for one and at the end of the over the batsmen appealed against the light. The umpires agreed and I heaved a sigh of relief.

My first day of Championship cricket was over. Although I'd done no more than field for two or three hours, I felt utterly exhausted, as if I personally had stopped every ball: mentally I had!

Rain was still in the air on the Thursday morning, but the forecast was set fair. With half a day lost, the captains, if this had been a 1992 match, would have been weighing up the possibility of mutual declarations in order to produce a definite result at five thirty on Friday. Twenty years ago this didn't happen too often. All things being equal Bolus would choose to bat all day and try to build a good first innings lead.

The young left arm fast bowler, John Lever, soon took care of our nightwatchman when play began on the second day. Boyce trapped Mike Smedley leg before without a run to his name and soon afterwards removed Bob White the same way. Our hopes of a first innings lead looked slim with the score four for 42. The batting bonus points system at that time operated only for the first 85 overs and a team received one point for every 25 runs made above 150.

Essex going out to bat.

Gary Sobers joined Brian Bolus at the wicket. If they failed we were in real trouble. They batted through to lunch. When Gary had been captain in 1971, he had found me a very useful ally. Having a reputation as a good fielder, more often than not I was given the duties as 12th man. One of the main duties of this office was not, as you might expect, running on the field in emergency, but running out of the ground!

Gary was fond of the horses and studied form before each race. It was the 12th man's job to nip up the road to the bookie's and place Gary's bet. No one could whip round to the bookmakers and back to the dressing room as quickly as I could. In 1971 my ability to field came second to my speed in the opposite direction. Oddly enough it was at the start of the 1972 season that I acquired the nickname, 'Arkle'.

Nothing to do with Gary and his bets. John Barnwell from Nottingham Forest had been recruited to give us some training before the season began. One of the routines involved running out of the ground and then along the side of the Trent. When I had finished the run first, for the umpteenth time, Bob White had chimed in with:

''How d'you manage it, Arkle?''

The name stuck. I'm better known in the dressing room now as 'Rags', but that came a year or two later.

The partnership between Bolus and Sobers continued after lunch. I had my pads on, but Basher Hassan was the next man in. The twitches attacked me again. I suppose I was fortunate it wasn't hayfever. I had terrible hayfever but the season for it was still a month away. There were times when I could do little more than stay indoors to avoid the pollen. I remember being struck down in the middle of a match and being incapable of fielding on the last day. Today modern drugs keep it under control.

I went out of the dressing room and found one of my mates who'd come from Retford. We went to the side of the hospitality tent and he bowled at me, trying to remove the tension that was building up.

It wasn't long before Sobers became another lbw victim. Basher Hassan went in. A year or two later Basher and I were to form a fielding partnership. He stood bravely at bat-pad whilst I took the close in position on the off side. Stuart Turner had dismissed Sobers. Turner never really hit the headlines but he performed very well for Essex especially in Sunday matches. Basher quickly hit him to the boundary for four. 'Tonker' Taylor, the Essex captain and wicketkeeper, was determined to keep the pressure up, bringing back Lever. Basher looked unhappy. He could only score the odd single. He reached 17, then became yet another lbw.

The total was six for 126—a lead of seven. Brian Bolus who had survived at the other end said something like, 'Take your time,' as I reached the wicket. He'd picked me for the side. I suppose he wanted to prove himself right, just as much as I did. It was before the days of 'sledging', but my mind was so concentrated that I don't think any amount of outside comment or noise would have disturbed me.

I survived Lever's first delivery—it was the final ball of the over. Bolus was then very careful to take as much of Lever's bowling as possible, leaving me to find my feet against the less lethal Edmeades.

I gauged the pace of the wicket, my tensed muscles relaxed. A couple of overs later I hoiked Edmeades for six into the adjoining cemetery. Taylor switched to an all spin attack of Robin Hobbs and Ray East.

I went with Ray East on a short tour of the West Indies organised by Titchener-Barrett a couple of years later. The tour was a light-hearted affair and very enjoyable. East was renowned as a comic; a talented left-arm spinner he was unlucky not to play for England. I recall, I think it was in Barbados, we climbed into a beach buggy which we thought was included as part of our visit and enjoyed a night out. Returning to the hotel however we were greeted by an irate customer who had booked the beach buggy for the evening and was left stranded.

The leg breaks of Hobbs and left arm spin of East caused me few problems and I hit both bowlers into the cemetery. The partnership with Bolus had added 80 when East had the captain caught. Mike Taylor came in at no.9. If I was going to make a reasonable score, I had to continue hitting out. We added another 52 for the 8th wicket, then Boyce returned and I hit out once too often. We were all out for 277.

Digging out Mum's scrapbook, I find the report notes:

''Randall, playing his first County Championship innings, showed all the confidence and composure of a mature batsman in his 140 minute innings. During that time he made Essex wilt, stroking and driving his way past half a century, with five sixes and four fours.''

On the final day the wicket eased. Edmeades, the Essex opener, played a dead bat to almost everything. He found an ally in Keith Fletcher and once they were settled in, the match drifted to a draw. Once the innings defeat was avoided, the spectators began to drift away. As I love fielding I was quite happy to continue for as long as the game carried on.

At that time Ladbroke's gave a cheque for £30 to the 'Man of the Match'. In front of a handful of spectators outside the pavilion, I was handed the Award. It was an extra bonus, but my 78 runs mattered so much more.

NOTTINGHAMSHIRE v ESSEX

Played on the RHP Ground, Newark, May 31, June 1 and 2, 1972
Match Drawn. Notts 7 pts, Essex 3 pts.

ESSEX

1	B.E.A. Edmeades	lbw b Stead	13	c Harris b Stead	89
2	G.J. Saville	b Sobers	2	(3) c Smedley b Stead	28
3	K.W.R. Fletcher	c Smedley b M.N.S. Taylor	42	(4) c Smedley b W. Taylor	68
4	B. Ward	lbw b Sobers	1	(5) c Pullan b Stead	1
5	K.D. Boyce	lbw b W. Taylor	25	(6) lbw b Stead	14
6	*+B. Taylor	b M.N.S. Taylor	6	(7) c Hassan b Stead	2
7	S. Turner	c Harris b M.N.S. Taylor	0	(9) not out	4
8	R.N.S. Hobbs	c Smedley b W. Taylor	1	not out	2
9	R.E. East	c M.N.S. Taylor b W. Taylor	18	(2) b Sobers	10
10	J.K. Lever	c Pullan b W. Taylor	0		
11	D.L. Acfield	not out	5		
	Extras	lb 3, nb 3	6	b 6, lb 5, w 2, nb 5	18
	Total		119	(7 wkts)	236

1-9 2-21 3-36 4-88 5-88 6-94 7-96 8-96 9-106

1-22 2-78 3-205 4-205 5-220 6-226 7-229

Bowling	O	M	R	W	O	M	R	W
Sobers	15	4	39	2	9	2	24	1
Stead	9	5	20	1	25	8	43	5
M.N.S. Taylor	14	4	35	3	16	3	38	0
W. Taylor	8.1	2	19	4	19	5	49	1
White					20	6	29	0
Harris					13	3	35	0

NOTTINGHAMSHIRE

1	M.J. Harris	lbw b Boyce	0
2	R.A. White	lbw b Boyce	24
3	+D.A. Pullan	c Taylor b Lever	3
4	M.J. Smedley	lbw b Boyce	0
5	*J.B. Bolus	c Turner b East	78
6	G.St A. Sobers	lbw b Turner	32
7	S.B. Hassan	lbw b Lever	17
8	D.W. Randall	c Ward b Boyce	78
9	M.N.S. Taylor	not out	17
10	B. Stead	c Hobbs b Boyce	2
11	W. Taylor	c Turner b Lever	6
	Extras	b 7, lb 9, nb 4	20
	Total		277

1-0 2-3 3-8 4-42 5-92 6-126 7-206 8-258 9-266

Bowling	O	M	R	W
Boyce	25	5	65	5
Lever	23	7	57	3
Turner	18	2	43	1
Edmeades	10	2	23	0
Hobbs	14	3	36	0
East	12	4	33	1

Umpires: P.B. Wight and H.D. Bird

Toss: Essex

Close of Play: 1st day: Notts 1-1 (White 0*, Pullan 0*); 2nd day: Essex (2) 4-0 (Edmeades 0*, East 4*).

CHAPTER 4

A Gold Medal

''New cricket starlet Derek Randall brought Lancashire back to earth with a bump as they threatened to overwhelm Notts in the Benson & Hedges Cup game at Trent Bridge. He did so well Notts ran out shock winners by 22 runs.''

That was how *The Sun* newspaper carried the story after we beat Lancashire in the second B&H match of 1973. Notts were in the North Zone of the Competition with Lancashire, Yorkshire, Derbyshire and Minor Counties (North), and if Notts were to progress to the knock-out section, then Lancashire were the side to beat. They had been the One Day Champions in 1972, having won the Gillette Cup and then beaten Kent, Sunday League winners, in a Champion of Champions Match.

During the second half of 1972 I had gained a regular place in the county First Eleven. Michael Austin reviewed the county's performance at the end of the summer and commented:

''Randall marked his debut with 78 against Essex at Newark. Since then, the unassuming 21-year-old from Retford has been eager to learn and typifies the attitude of Notts youngsters. 'I could play cricket for ever' Randall told me recently. His lightning swoops, pick-ups and throws staggered many county batsmen and his efforts in the field spotlighted the slowness of

Batting in my long hair days.

some team mates. Notts badly needed someone of Randall's reliability close to the wicket.''

It seemed as if I had a future in county cricket, but the unpredictability of a cricketing career was very quickly illustrated at the end of season get-together of players and the County Committee. The Chairman announced that two of the senior men, Brian Bolus and Mike Taylor, would not be having their contracts renewed for 1973; also not retained was Peter Plummer the slow left arm bowler who had been on the staff for five years. I hasten to add that today life is not quite so brutal and players do get more notice before being sacked. The announcement put a damper on the party.

Mike Taylor moved to Hampshire and spent the next eight years in their First Eleven. He is now the Marketing Manager for that county. Brian Bolus moved across the border to Derbyshire, being appointed as their captain. Peter Plummer went on to play in Minor Counties cricket.

Before the 1973 season began Gary Sobers was re-appointed as county captain. For the first time in many years he had not played international cricket during the winter and it was hoped he would be fresh and fit to lead Notts; he did not turn up at Trent Bridge until a day or two before the start of county matches and Mike Smedley, our new vice-captain took charge of the pre-season preparation helped by John Barnwell and Dusty Hare, plus Trevor Tunnicliffe, the Loughborough University student, who had now joined the staff.

Our opening game was at Derby in the Benson & Hedges Cup. A terrible draught seems to blow whenever we visit that former racecourse. The ground is so wide open that there's nowhere to hide from the wind. Even worse there was, then, little to stop the ball going miles over the boundary. In that respect I am reminded of Adelaide. That Australia ground is always compared with Worcester, but it is one of the longest and thinnest grounds on which I have played. If a batsman hits the ball straight, it takes about four fieldsmen to return the ball to the wicketkeeper.

Conditions at Derby in the early '70s were rather primitive—tin baths and the ever present wind whistling through holes in the timberwork. Derbyshire have built up a reputation for fast bowlers and 1973, with Mike Hendrick and Alan Ward, was no exception.

Our Championship games against them at that time were played on the Rutland Ground at Ilkeston and it was there, either in 1973 or the following summer, that I watched one of the best hundreds I ever witnessed. Gary Sobers, when no one else could lay a bat on Hendrick or Ward, toyed with the bowling and seemed to be in no trouble at all. The game was a particularly irritating one for me. I played forward to a ball from Geoff Miller and was hit on the pad. The ball went up in the air. I moved out of the way to avoid being hit on the head as it descended. The wind blew at a vital moment and the ball landed right on top of the bails.

Sorry, I seem to have been side-tracked. Sobers won the toss in the 1973 B&H game and decided to bat. Pasty Harris, who had scarcely made a run in 1972, went straight into the attack, hitting 18 of the first 22 runs. He was then clean bowled by Ward. Going in first wicket down, I managed to run myself out. Only Mike Smedley made worthwhile runs. The score fell to 140 for nine. Bill Taylor brought some Mancunian pressure to bear and as last man hit a quick 17, so we finished with a modest 164 for nine off the 55 overs.

Brian Bolus was leading Derbyshire and determined to show Notts how wrong they had been in releasing him. Barry Stead was at his most raucous. He appealed for lbw against Bolus four times in as many overs and on the last occasion the umpire agreed with him. Stead also dismissed Page and Borrington. Derbyshire were 15 for three. In four overs Stead had picked up three wickets. Clive Inman, who had moved from Leicestershire during the close season, was the one batsman to survive more than a few overs. We won by 33 runs.

The fixtures were a little odd that summer. Having played a single B&H game, we did nothing for nearly a fortnight, when the first Sunday League match took place at Trent Bridge. We batted first. Basher Hassan had been promoted to open with Mike Harris and fifty was added for the first wicket. I went in when Harris was lbw, then watched as Hassan, Smedley and Sobers all came and went with just fifteen runs added. The total reached 70 for four. I sent a simple catch to Rocker Robinson at mid on, but he misjudged the ball and I celebrated by hitting the next delivery for six. My score of 32 was the highest of the innings, Notts' total being just 134.

Boycott then demonstrated how to deal with a seamers' wicket. He made a commanding 72 and Yorkshire won by seven wickets. If you want someone to bat for your life, get Boycott. He is a great technician with massive concentration, but I was surprised when I read that he had been selected to coach the England team. He seems to believe that every young batsman has the same mentality as himself. On tour in New Zealand he tried to sort out my problems, but his style of play was totally alien to me and he had to abandon his efforts which were just having the opposite effect to that intended. I remember playing against Yorkshire at Bradford and saying to young Graham Stevenson, "You watch Boycott, I bet I'll run him out."

Boycott liked quick singles and was batting with Jim Love, who rather trundled between the wickets. I waited my opportunity. It was not long before Boycott drove the ball into the covers. I anticipated his shot and had the ball in before Boycott could make his ground. Afterwards Boycott had a go at Stevenson, who rather foolishly told Geoffrey that I was determined to run him out. "Why didn't you warn me?"

Boycott did not put the power into his shots to pierce the field and in fact preferred to score in singles. Most people think of Boycott as a dour defensive player, but he could score quickly when in the mood, as was proved in some of the One Day Internationals in Australia. Mainly however he got so het-up with his own game that he appeared to play as much for his average as for the side, which was silly because his talent was such that he could master any bowling.

He should never have been made captain of England, since he doesn't mix easily with other players. Having said that I remember an occasion in Pakistan when I was feeling particularly low and was missing English food. Boycott took me out and found a restaurant that served roast beef and Yorkshire Pudding. It was a great night out and really cheered me up. So he wasn't always as self-centred as is made out. If he dared to be a little more adventurous, he would have been an even greater batsman.

The day following our defeat at the hands of Yorkshire came the Benson & Hedges contest with Lancashire, also at Trent Bridge. Gary Sobers won the toss and elected to bat. I should add against his will. Sobers was very quick to size up the tactics for One Day cricket when it was introduced and was sure that, on winning the toss, a side should field first. He talked about this in the dressing room, but the Notts team persuaded him that batting first was best. I wondered why, but I realised that batsmen are likely to vote to bat first, bowlers will normally disagree, but in any given team there are more specialist batsmen than bowlers!

Peter Lever and Leapy Lee were the Lancashire opening attack. Lever was at that time in the England side. Watching him from the ring gave a deceptive impression because he was not as fast as his run up suggested. His action was somewhat ungainly, but he made the ball move in the air and was very accurate. Lee had originally played for Northants, but moved to Lancashire the previous summer. In 1973 he was destined to capture more than 100 wickets. I feel he was unlucky not to be given an opportunity with England.

Harris and Hassan never looked comfortable, playing and missing as they were beaten by the movement off the wicket. Harris located gaps in the off side field, but was caught low down at mid wicket by Clive Lloyd when he had reached 26. Hassan was out two runs later. Lee and Lever had given way to the left arm spin of David Hughes and Barry Wood's medium pace when I came in. A four off Hughes gave me confidence and I soon was timing the ball well. Mike Smedley did not survive long. Lloyd brought on Simmons with his off breaks. I find off spinners the easiest type of bowler to combat, but Simmons was a very experienced bowler and the over before lunch had me leg before for 56. We were then 137 for four off 38 overs. Sobers was still batting. We hoped he would take the bowling apart after the break, but he was run out and our total after 55 overs was 179 for eight.

Harold Rhodes had been signed up for Notts for One Day games only. Rhodes had been a major part of the Derbyshire attack but had been a controversial figure due to his bowling action. He opened the Notts bowling with Barry Stead. Lancashire found runs very hard to obtain. Barry had 12 runs hit off his six over spell, Harold Rhodes conceded only 11. I had batted in the pre-season nets quite regularly against Rhodes and I don't recall a bowler who made the ball jag back as much as he did.

Bob White and Bill Taylor took over the attack, but the run rate scarcely increased. Taylor had David Lloyd caught in the slips. Sobers put himself on and removed Barry Wood.

32 overs had gone and the score was 86 for two. Clive Lloyd strode to the crease. It was up to him to get the scoring rate moving. At the opposite end was the contrasting figure of Harry Pilling. Pilling obtained his runs with nudges, usually singles. Lloyd, who was about a foot taller than Pilling had unbelievable power. He was the arch exponent of positive cricket. On the field he was a hard professional; he wouldn't give anything away. He was keen to win, but just as big a man when he lost. Off the field he would give anyone the time of day.

He had been in just a few minutes when he played a ball on the off side and started to run. He failed to appreciate that I'd out-thought him and was moving towards the ball almost as it left his bat. He caught sight of me and turned to regain his crease, but too late. My throw hit the stumps.

A few overs later I rather luckily ran out Lancashire's other overseas player, the wicketkeeper, Farook Engineer. The Indian had not got off the mark, when he was hit on the pads by a ball from Barry Stead. Engineer moved forward quickly, no doubt to make certain the umpire gave him the benefit of the doubt as Stead bellowed: "Owzat?"

The ball bounded in my direction and I had the wicket broken before Engineer could scramble to safety. Lancashire were now 92 for five. Sullivan made a brave attempt to save the match, hitting Rhodes for two fours and a six in one over. The score rose to 149 for five. 31 runs were required from the last five overs.

Gary Sobers was not going to let the game slip away and brought himself on for a second spell. Sullivan drove the first delivery straight to me at cover. The tail collapsed and Notts won by 22 runs. Jim Laker presented me with the Man of The Match Award. The first such medal I ever received.

The *Daily Telegraph's* report noted:

"Randall ran out Lancashire's two key batsmen and later caught the aggressive Sullivan with an alertness and skill which underlined his qualities as a first-class fielder ... Randall's innings earlier in the day was significant for its controlled aggression, judgment and, above all, footwork. In 70 minutes he made 56 glorious runs, including 10 fours."

Our third game in the B&H competition was against Minor Counties North. Basher Hassan made a big score and we had no problem beating them. Chris Old's brother, Alan, better known on the Rugby field, opened their bowling. He was a useful performer, but nothing like as good as Chris.

The final match in the series began on rather a sad note. Arthur Wheat, who had been the Notts scorer for many years, died just prior to the game. A wicketkeeper, he would tell us stories of the days when he kept to Larwood and Voce, as well as life on the Trent Bridge staff in the 1920s and 1930s. His fingers were gnarled and twisted from his cricketing days. Bill Thornley took over as scorer for the Yorkshire match and, like Arthur Wheat, he was to continue in office until his death.

The Yorkshire game was on the vast expanse of Hull's

ground. These one day games have sometimes proved a mathematician's delight and this match was a perfect example. We didn't have to win the game to go through to the knock-out section of the competition, all that mattered was our 'strike-rate', that's to say our runs per wicket. Gary Sobers won the toss again and, this time we were all agreed we had to bat first.

Harris and Hassan opened the batting and carried out their orders to the letter. They batted until the 53rd over, adding 199 runs in the process. Our total was 208 for two. Yorkshire made 209 for two and collected three points. Our strike rate—there being three teams level on points at the top of the table—took us into the quarter finals.

We were drawn against Worcestershire at New Road—a beautiful setting for cricket, but at that time the facilities were not the best. Jack, the dressing room attendant, served the players' meals in the dressing room. It was a custom I was to meet again in Pakistan, but not quite for the same reasons.

Worcestershire were led by Norman Gifford. He's a bowler who would try every trick in the book to get batsmen out; his favourite, which diddled new recruits to county cricket, was to bowl before the batsman was ready. I've had quite a few battles with him, and a few words, but in a good natured way. Their other main bowler was the West Indian, Vanburn Holder, perhaps not so well remembered as Marshall, Holding and Garner, but very effective in county cricket.

We lost the toss. Worcestershire batted and Ron Headley played a brilliant innings of 84. Alan Ormrod hit a brisk 54 and the total reached 234 for eight. We had decided to leave out our regular wicketkeeper, Dave Pullan, use Mike Harris behind the stumps and bring in Trevor Tunnicliffe. Trevor proved his worth with a very good first spell of six overs for eight runs, but then suffered under the blows of Ormrod.

After their great batting feat against Yorkshire, our openers came down to earth with a bump. Basher was lbw to the third ball—bowled by Holder. The same bowler removed Harris in his

Norman Gifford, a bowler with more than one trick up his sleeve.

next over. Smedley went quickly and I clung on whilst Sobers tried to save the day. Gifford set a very defensive field—it was in the days before fielding circles. Sobers therefore had difficulty reaching the boundary. His knees were causing him problems, so quick singles, which would have been the answer, were out of the question. It was more than my life was worth to run Gary out! I survived some seven overs for half a dozen runs. Sobers managed 36, then mistimed a sweep and was caught by Yardley off Gifford. Bob White batted out the innings, but we never looked like reaching the target and the game was lost by 89 runs. Worcestershire went on to the Final that summer, but lost at Lord's to Kent.

I did get my revenge over Worcestershire later in the year. The Championship match at New Road was the scene of my first hundred for Notts. This is such a milestone in any cricketer's life, that perhaps the reader will forgive a description of the circumstances. We'd had a terrible time all year and were firmly fixed at the foot of the table with just one win in 18 fixtures. There were two matches left when we met Worcestershire, who were well up in the top half of the championship. The home side batted first and Glenn Turner, the New Zealand Test player, just launched straight into the attack. He reached a hundred before lunch. Worcester declared at 382 for eight. On the second day our batting failed miserably—all out 132 with a deficit of 250. I should add that both Harris and Hassan were absent with injuries. Paul Todd opened the innings with Bob White. Their first wicket partnership failed to produce a run. When the follow on was enforced, they managed a single before Todd was dismissed by Brian Brain. I came in to join White. There was still half the afternoon to go and Worcestershire were looking for a two day win.

Vanburn Holder was not playing, being in the West Indies touring side, but in his place was a promising young all-rounder, Imran Khan. I was lucky not to be caught early on, but quickly found the ball hitting the middle of the bat and for once gauging the spin of Gifford I hit 107 in something under an hour and half. We lost the game by nine wickets, but at least reached 357 in our second innings.

The press commented that my innings was a reminder to the Test selectors who were to choose the England team for the West Indies the following week. It was nice to know that I had friends among the journalists, but I feel they were a trifle optimistic. My only taste of 'international' cricket to date was playing for Young England against West Indies at Old Trafford six weeks earlier.

The rain poured down—no play on the first day, only two hours on the second. Rohan Kanhai, the West Indies captain, made a very generous declaration on the third morning with the touring team's total 137 for three. I shall let Clive Taylor's report tell the story:

"Smashed into a state of bewilderment, Young England were saved from becoming joke figures at Old Trafford by the batting of Derek Randall and David Bairstow, two players whose Test careers are further off than most of the others in the side. They

David Bairstow, for once, looks more surprised than I do.

came together when the senior contenders had gone in an opening assault by Grayson Shillingford, easily the fastest of the West Indies bowlers and ironically the one least likely to play against England on Thursday. The score was 38 for five, Shillingford had got four and Young England were looking decidedly aged. Then Randall of Notts in only his second full season, and already a fine-looking prospect, partnered Bairstow in a stand of 93 in 85 minutes."

Bairstow and I have had a love-hate relationship ever since. He makes a bee line for me when he comes to Trent Bridge. If I don't see him coming, my neck is suddenly in a 'friendly' arm-lock which disables me until the lunch interval. During away games in Yorkshire I was always forced to guard my 'coffin', since 'Bluey' would adjust my gear and I'd either spend half the match unravelling it or trying to locate the bits that had disappeared. The county circuit's not been the same since he retired.

September 1973 was altogether a month to remember—my hundred had been scored on the 3rd of the month, on the 11th, during the final match of the summer, I was awarded my County Cap and on Saturday September 29th, I made the most sensible decision of my life and married Liz.

NOTTINGHAMSHIRE v LANCASHIRE

Played on the Trent Bridge Ground, Nottingham, May 7, 1973
Nottinghamshire beat Lancashire by 22 runs.

NOTTINGHAMSHIRE

1	M.J. Harris	c C.H. Lloyd b Hughes	26
2	S.B. Hassan	st Engineer b Wood	18
3	D.W. Randall	lbw b Simmons	56
4	M.J. Smedley	c Simmons b Hughes	15
5	*G.St A. Sobers	run out	22
6	G. Frost	lbw b Simmons	2
7	R.A. White	not out	25
8	B. Stead	c Wood b Lever	5
9	H.J. Rhodes	run out	6
10	+D.A. Pullan		
11	W. Taylor		
	Extras	lb 3, nb 1	4
Total		(8 wkts, 55 overs)	179

1-43 2-45 3-82 4-137 5-138 6-140 7-150 8-179

Bowling	O	M	R	W
Lever	11	3	32	1
Lee	9	1	31	0
Hughes	11	0	34	2
Wood	10	1	28	1
Simmons	11	1	31	2
Sullivan	3	0	19	0

LANCASHIRE

1	B. Wood	c Stead b Sobers	49
2	*D. Lloyd	c Harris b Taylor	14
3	H. Pilling	b Stead	18
4	C.H. Lloyd	run out	1
5	F.C. Hayes	c Hassan b Rhodes	21
6	+F.M. Engineer	run out	0
7	J. Sullivan	c Randall b Sobers	36
8	D.P. Hughes	c Sobers b Rhodes	0
9	J. Simmons	lbw b Rhodes	1
10	P. Lever	b Taylor	3
11	P.G. Lee	not out	2
	Extras	b 4, lb 6, nb 2	12
Total		(53.1 overs)	157

1-37 2-86 3-88 4-92 5-92 6-149 7-151 8-151 9-153

Bowling	O	M	R	W
Stead	11	4	18	1
Taylor	10.1	3	19	2
Rhodes	11	2	47	3
White	9	0	36	0
Sobers	10	3	17	2
Frost	2	0	8	0

Umpires: C.S. Elliott and H. Horton

CHAPTER 5

A Great Day at Lord's

The fast bowling of Holding, Roberts, Daniel and Holder had crushed England in the Test Series of 1976. Four matches lost and the game at Lord's drawn due to rain. Two summers had gone by since I had won my County Cap. In 1974 I couldn't do anything right, the Test selectors who had been keeping an eye on me despaired.

"You won't play for England unless you can prove to the selectors that you can build an innings. Scores of thirty or forty may be of use to Notts, but they don't catch the selectorial eye."

That kind of comment was made to me fairly often. Things went much better in 1975 and a pleasant trip to South Africa with Robins' Team the following winter kept me in trim for 1976. Near the start of the season I was picked for the M.C.C. team to play West Indies at Lord's—it was the modern version of a Test Trial, the home side being composed of a mixture of England players and young hopefuls.

Some idea of the confidence that Clive Lloyd had in his bowlers can be seen from the fact that he declared the West Indies innings closed on the first day at the modest total of 251 for nine, with Deryck Murray batting well, not out 33. I scored a single in the M.C.C. total of 197—like the rest of the team I was rather distracted when Dennis Amiss was badly injured early in the innings, being hit on the head by a ball from Holding. The wound required four stitches before Amiss could resume. Viv Richards hit a glorious hundred in West Indies second innings and needing 302 to win on the final day, M.C.C. fell apart, all out 83, of which I made 5. Of the eleven members of that M.C.C. side only one, Mike Brearley, was picked the following weekend to represent England in the First Test.

Disappointed by my failure, I determined to make runs for Notts. Against Kent, who, in Jarvis, Shepherd, Woolmer and Underwood, had an attack not far below Test standard, I hit 164. At the end of July I made 204 not out off the Somerset bowlers. Not up to Kent's standard it's true, but they did have the West Indian Moseley and a young tearaway called Ian Botham.

I had been picked as England's 12th man in a couple of the Tests. When the series was ended the selectors met to choose a fourteen man squad for the three One Day Internationals scheduled for the last week of August.

Listening to the radio, I heard the list of names chosen. The selectors had dumped the old hands, who had failed in the Tests, and decided to give youth a chance. I was picked together with Graham Gooch, Graham Barlow and Ian Botham. Of course I might well end up as 12th man again—the one disadvantage of being a good fielder, you always make an ideal sub.

I went with the Notts side for four days by the sea—we were playing Sussex at Hove. On the Saturday I was quickly dismissed by the England captain, Tony Greig, and went back to the pavilion to watch what turned out to be one of the best innings of the year. Clive Rice, who was in his second season with us, hit 246 in about 300 minutes. Notts next best scorer was Mike Smedley, who made 44. Rice's innings was compared, in the press, with Ted Alletson's. I'm not much of a one for history, but Alletson is a legend at Trent Bridge. A cricketer from Welbeck who is reputed to have hit the fastest innings of all time for Notts against Sussex at Hove a few years before the First World War. Notts won the

Clive Rice hit 246 in 300 minutes at Hove.

Championship game by 86 runs, but I must admit that on the final day, the Tuesday, my mind was on the long journey to Scarborough, ready for the First One Day International which was to start on Thursday. Tony Greig had a badly bruised finger and was forced to stand down as England captain, Alan Knott taking his place. Robin Jackman and myself were also omitted from the final England eleven.

As in the Tests, England were completely outplayed. The one batsman to achieve anything was Graham Barlow. He made 80, the next best being Amiss's 34. Barlow was a very strong, very fit left hander. His county career had begun a couple of years before mine. He had been at Loughborough and trained as a P.E. teacher. Unfortunately his cricket was to come to a premature end due to back trouble. You wouldn't have believed, seeing him in the 1970s, that someone so clearly as fit as Barlow would be forced to retire due to a back strain. We were similar players, hitting the ball hard and enjoying the physical side of fielding. On tour he and I were normally mid wicket and cover. Later of course David Gower took over Barlow's place in the field. Middlesex could have done with Barlow's batting over recent summers—in 1976 it seemed as if our careers would run in tandem, but it was not to be. To see Barlow today, you would hardly recognise the athletic figure who saved England's face at Scarborough.

The One Day cricket circus travelled from the Yorkshire coast to London for the second match of the series, at Lord's. The failures at Scarborough meant that the three 12th men were all included in the Lord's eleven. Greig, Jackman and myself replaced Botham, John Lever and David Steele.

1976 had been a particularly dry summer, but the one rainy spell had coincided with the Lord's Test. The England team were now back at Lord's and so was the rain. The match was a sell out, but the crowd only saw about half a day's play on the Saturday. At Scarborough England had batted first; this time, West Indies took first strike. Mike Hendrick, perhaps the best bowler England have had for One Day matches, dismissed both the West Indian

Graham Barlow contending with me for an England place.

openers, Fredericks and Greenidge. Mike was later to join Notts, but like Barlow his career was ended too early due to injury.

Viv Richards, as in the Scarborough game, soon put a smile back on West Indian faces. He made 97 and the West Indies reached 221 off 47.5 overs—the match, due to a delayed start, had been reduced to 50 overs per side.

There had been one or two showers during the afternoon, then just before England went in to bat, a real cloudburst descended, wetting the wicket as the ground staff tried to rush the covers on. It was late in the day—after six o'clock—when our innings finally began. Barry Wood and Dennis Amiss opened, as in the first match. Playing on the Edgbaston pitch had helped Amiss to become a very competent batsman; if the batting wickets didn't help him, certainly the example of the West Indians Kanhai and Kallicharran did. He had played Test cricket since 1966, but had not been picked for the 1976 series until the Fifth Test at The Oval. Here Amiss showed his class, hitting a great 203. Later I recall watching him score his hundred at Delhi. He was a player with plenty of guts and determination.

Barry Wood's was the first wicket to fall. A vicious ball from Andy Roberts, just short of a length, rose and hit Wood's hand, or the bat handle. The ball bounced off to give the bowler a fairly easy catch. Poor Wood had lasted less than an over: he had gone in the first over at Scarborough too.

By the time the umpires pulled up the stumps on Saturday night, England were 47 for four. Roberts had taken all four wickets—Wood, Amiss, Woolmer, and Barlow. I had gone in when Barlow was out—like Wood he had been caught off the handle. I somehow managed to survive the final few deliveries before the close. Graham Gooch was my surviving partner.

Gooch had been tried in the Test series of 1975 against Australia. He was then only 21 and had the embarrassment of failing to score in both innings. He did little better in the Second Test of 1975 and was then left out. A dedicated batsman he had determined to overcome his weaknesses and received a lot of help and advice from Kenny McEwan, who at that time opened the Essex batting. Gooch had been ignored for all the 1976 Tests and like myself had the opportunity of proving himself in these One Day Internationals. As it happened he failed again and it was not until the 1978 season, with Tests against Pakistan and New Zealand, that he was able to demonstrate his skills again.

Play resumed on Sunday afternoon. Instead of Saturday's full house, about three quarters of the seats were unoccupied. I can't blame the spectators for staying away. The weather was still damp and miserable. Our best batsmen had been disposed of in 14 overs, it seemed unlikely that the remaining six would last above an hour.

This opinion was reinforced when Vanburn Holder opened the bowling and off his fourth delivery had Gooch caught at the wicket. Tony Greig, our skipper, joined me. He had been completely out of form with the bat all summer. He scratched about for three runs, then a ball from Bernard Julien hit the top edge of his bat and flew high in the air to square leg where it was gobbled up by Viv Richards. The scoreboard read 62 for six.

Alan Knott abandoned his cup of tea and walked purposely to the crease. A very quiet, well-mannered man he was a master of the wicketkeeping craft. He was a batsman for a crisis. He was also a cricketer of vast experience. He had around eighty Test appearances to his name, but I doubt if he had come in to bat many times before with England in such a state.

Despite the grey skies and the eccentric bounce off the wicket, I felt comparatively relaxed. Effectively the pressure was off, the worst I could do was equal everyone else's dismal performance. I played the bowling of Julien and Holder with some confidence. Clive Lloyd—mum's favourite cricketer—brought on Collis King. I took advantage of his slower pace, hitting him off the back foot for four over long off, then hooking him for six.

The stand between Alan Knott and myself seemed to be well established when Knott was run out in a very unfortunate manner. I must interrupt here to say that I have on occasion been guilty of

Clive Lloyd, mum's favourite cricketer.

running out my partner, because I tend to think that he can run as quickly as I can. In this instance I was an innocent party. The bowler stopped a drive from me which had all the appearance of going to the boundary. Alan had started off for a run. The bowler swivelled round and broke the wicket with Alan a couple of yards adrift.

Robin Jackman came in. Jackman had been playing for Surrey for over ten years mainly as seam bowler, but he was also a useful, if unconventional batsman. He was an ideal limited overs cricketer. It became clear that a change of bowling would be needed to give the West Indies a breakthrough. Lloyd brought back Andy Roberts. My response was to hit him for two fours off a single over. A year or two later I wouldn't have been so bold.

Notts went to Dean Park, Bournemouth, to play Hampshire, when Roberts was in their side. I was batting when Barry Stead came in. Roberts responded by giving Barry a bouncer. The cheeky, or should I say, foolhardy, Yorkshireman, hooked the ball to the boundary.

Barry winks to me. "What about that for a shot?"

I wince, rather than wink and out of the corner of my mouth reply:

"Watch out for the next one, Barry."

Roberts favourite tactic was to bowl, by his standards, a slow bouncer, then follow it up with one that went like lightning. This time his second delivery fractured Barry's jaw. Yorkshiremen are generally an obstinate lot and Barry could be an awkward cuss even by their standards. He was all for continuing his innings and attempting to hit the next one for four. I did manage to persuade him that it would be more sensible to leave, while he could still manage it under his own steam.

I'm not certain how I got diverted into that yarn—there used to be some commentator on the wireless when I was young, who would forget for a moment that he was reporting on a match and would launch into some tale; as I was trying to hear what happened to Cowdrey or Barrington, he used to drive me potty.

Back to the action:

The England score was moving healthily upwards and it was beginning to be worthwhile trying to work out how many runs per over we wanted for victory. I was lucky not to be caught by Viv Richards when I had made 61, but I think that was about the only real chance I gave. Lloyd was keeping his two main strike bowlers, Roberts and Holding back for the final four overs—they each had two left. Then Holder clean bowled Jackman. 42 runs were required off the last six overs.

Derek Underwood came in at no.10. Lloyd brought himself on to bowl. It was obvious that he was going to tempt me to hit out and get caught in the deep. I wasn't to be fooled and just scored four off his first over. By the time Lloyd started his second over, I'd forgotten my resolution and the first ball went in the direction of Collis King, who took a well-judged catch. I was out for 88. Two balls later Lloyd dismissed Underwood and the West Indies had won by 36 runs. It was just after four o'clock. Play that day had lasted 31.3 overs, so the crowd had had something for their money.

The next day there were some moans in the press that I ought to have had the Man of The Match award. It had been judged by Jack Bailey, Secretary of the M.C.C. Viv Richards was the recipient for his 97. I was happy enough.

West Indies had won the series two matches to nil, but England still had to go up to Edgbaston that night to play the third match due to start on Bank Holiday Monday. That was the theory, however torrential, or in Barry Stead language 'territorial', rain washed out play and it was not until the afternoon of Tuesday that the game began reduced to 32 overs. Bob Woolmer and Robin Jackman were dropped and Ian Botham and John Lever returned to the eleven. Lever gave us a brilliant start, when West Indies batted first. Fredericks was caught off the first ball of the match, then off his third ball, Lever had Viv Richards caught at point by Barry Wood. The West Indians weren't depressed by this terrible start. Greenidge and Lloyd soon put bat to ball. The outfield was very slippery after the rain, which made fielding difficult; the wet ball was no help to our bowlers. Runs came at about seven an over, only the mean length of Hendrick having any power to curb the flow. Botham's three overs went for 31 and Underwood's three for 28. The total was 223 for nine. We faced a formidable task, but Amiss and Wood gave us a sound opening partnership. The total rose to 54. Roberts and Holding had been seen off without a wicket falling. Then came Holder and Julien and a collapse. Julien clean bowled both openers, Holding dismissed Barlow for a duck and Gooch for three. I came in when Gooch's wicket fell. We were behind the run rate and the match, being restricted to 32 overs a side, was beyond hope. Greig failed. I managed to hit eight boundaries in a fairly quick 39 before being caught off Holder. The tail collapsed and West Indies won by 50 runs.

So Clive Lloyd's side had triumphed both in the Tests and the One Days. Flicking back through the scores of that tour I am reminded that though England failed to win a match against them, West Indies were defeated twice, both times by teams captained by Mike Brearley.

I was given the Award of England's Man of the Series for the One Day Internationals—Richards received the West Indian Award. It is interesting to read the report of the match with comments not only on myself but also another young hopeful:

"Perhaps the most useful contribution of the series to English cricket, apart from the £96,000 which it brought in, was the revelation that Randall was no means as confounded by fast bowling as appeared from his brief innings for M.C.C. at Lord's in May. A week ago he must have been some way down the list of possibles for the batting places in India. He has worked his way up since then ... Yesterday's match also gave Ian Botham a chance to play a few strokes in the closing stages. His batting has looked several classes better than his bowling in these matches, but it is easy to forget that he is still only 20."

That was Michael Melford writing in the *Daily Telegraph* and preserved in Mum's scrapbook.

ENGLAND v WEST INDIES

Played at Lord's, August 28 and 29, 1976
West Indies won by 36 runs.

WEST INDIES

1	R.C. Fredericks	c Randall b Hendrick	19
2	C.G. Greenidge	b Hendrick	29
3	I.V.A. Richards	c Woolmer b Greig	97
4	*C.H. Lloyd	c Barlow b Woolmer	27
5	C.L. King	c Wood b Woolmer	1
6	L.G. Rowe	b Underwood	4
7	+D.L. Murray	c and b Underwood	1
8	B.D. Julien	c Randall b Underwood	4
9	M.A. Holding	c Barlow b Wood	16
10	V.A. Holder	b Greig	2
11	A.M.E. Roberts	not out	7
	Extras	b 5, lb 5, w 1, nb 3	14
Total		(47.5 overs)	221

1-51 2-53 3-121 4-124 5-135 6-143 7-154 8-193 9-201

Bowling	O	M	R	W
Hendrick	9	2	34	2
Jackman	10	1	50	0
Woolmer	10	0	52	2
Underwood	10	2	27	3
Greig	5.5	0	31	2
Wood	3	0	13	1

ENGLAND

1	B. Wood	c and b Roberts	4
2	D.L. Amiss	c Murray b Roberts	12
3	R.A. Woolmer	b Roberts	9
4	G.D. Barlow	c Holder b Roberts	0
5	G.A. Gooch	c Murray b Holder	5
6	D.W. Randall	c King b Lloyd	88
7	*A.W. Greig	c Richards b Julien	3
8	+A.P.E. Knott	run out	22
9	R.D. Jackman	b Holder	14
10	D.L. Underwood	c Greenidge b Lloyd	2
11	M. Hendrick	not out	0
	Extras	lb 14, w 4, nb 8	26
Total		(45.3 overs)	185

1-4 2-25 3-30 4-31 5-48 6-62 7-125 8-180 9-185

Bowling	O	M	R	W
Roberts	8	1	27	4
Holding	8	0	26	0
Julien	10	4	22	1
Holder	10	0	35	2
King	8	0	45	0
Lloyd	1.3	0	4	2

Umpires: W.E. Alley and A.E. Fagg

CHAPTER 6

A Journey to India

Charlie Elliott, the old Derbyshire batsman and, in 1976, a Test Selector, had taken me on one side in the middle of the Lord's One Day International.

"You've proved you can field," he said. "Now prove you can bat."

I'd taken his advice in the One Day International. By coincidence the day after the One Days, West Indies came to Trent Bridge to play Notts. We batted first and after Nirmal Nanan was out for 2, Paul Todd and myself added 134 for the second wicket, seeing off the fast attack of Holding and Daniel—such was the strength of the West Indies bowling, that Daniel was not required for the One Day games. I scored 85 and 39 in this game, the highest score in each innings, vital runs, since I knew that three days after the match the selectors would gather to pick the England team to tour India.

That Monday was a long day. There was no county match. The selectors' meeting went on much longer than scheduled. Eventually the team was announced and my name was on it.

My previous tours abroad had been to South Africa—with Derrick Robins' side—and a couple of short trips to the West Indies. There could scarcely be a greater contrast between those

With Liz, packing my bags for India.

Tours and this visit to India. We flew from a miserable late November in England to a Bombay heat wave. The heat and the crowds. I'd never experienced anything like either before. More people turned out to watch our three days of net practice at the Wankhede Stadium than came to a county game in England. The crowds assembled outside our hotel and cheered those of the team they recognised from previous visits, notably of course Tony Greig, the captain, whose height and blond hair, made him immediately known. Greig liked India. He had put his foot in it at the start of the series against West Indies, when he announced to the press that England would make West Indies grovel. At his press conference on arrival in Bombay he chose his words with more care and in answer to a barbed question stated that he thought Indian umpires were the best in the world. I reckon that placed him on the right side of any number of doubtful decisions!

Our tour manager was Ken Barrington, the old Surrey and England batsman. He was what I would describe as a swashbuckler. He gave me plenty of good advice, some of which must have soaked in. On a later tour, when the Packer business was hitting the headlines, England sent Doug Insole as manager being more of a diplomat and demoted Ken to his assistant. The one thing they had in common was an ability to devour an orange in seconds.

Food was a major problem for all the players. In the hotel in Bombay we could get European dishes, but no sooner had we moved to Poona for the first match than both Barlow and Willis went down with a stomach bug. My turn was to come about a fortnight later just before the First Test. Bernard Thomas was officially our tour physio, but soon developed into the camp cook. He became an expert at bananas on toast and spam—this being a regular lunch time diet.

I must mention Dennis Amiss whilst I remember because he was my first room mate and helped me to get accustomed to life on tour. I managed to run myself out for a duck in the first game—Brearley made 202, Fletcher 118, Greig 162 and Tolchard

67. We declared for five wickets down. I did earn some complimentary remarks on my fielding and caught out Solkar, the local side's captain who was batting well and trying to earn himself a Test place.

By the time the second match was well under way, I had found that I had an affinity with the Indian spectators. They enjoyed my fielding and appreciated the odd cartwheel. On the final day of the match at Jaipur, where I was 12th man, I rather tired of lounging in the pavilion and took a stroll round the boundary. After signing an autograph or two and shaking a few hands, I adjusted a policeman's hat. The crowd began to laugh. Everyone seemed happy and light-hearted. Suddenly there was a shout from the middle. I turned to see that Geoff Cope had stopped bowling and was gesticulating in my direction. I returned to the pavilion. The fact of the matter was that my antics were causing more interest with the spectators than the game itself and Geoff and the captain were not too pleased.

Cope used to field very close to bat, not because he was particularly brave, but because he was so short sighted, the position didn't seem to worry him. A week after the game at Jaipur the news came that Geoff Cope's father had died suddenly and Geoff had to fly home.

We flew to Delhi for the First Test—according to the press Tony Greig stated: "I smell victory," as he stepped from the aircraft, but it was the written rather than spoken word which grabbed the headlines on the eve of the game. To the amazement of the English team, Sunil Gavaskar, the leading Indian batsman, published a book which criticised several of his fellow Test players in no uncertain terms and accused the Indian manager, Ramchand, of misrepresentation.

India were therefore in a state of disarray. Amiss played a careful innings of 179 and Knott hit 75 in the England total of 381. Lever was easily the best of our bowlers; Old and Willis were innocuous. Lever took seven for 46 and India collapsed to 122 all out. Gavaskar batted well in the second innings, but only fog on the fourth morning and bad light the same evening prevented us winning with a day to spare. As it was the match finished after 30 minutes on the fifth day. We won by an innings.

We spent Christmas in Calcutta with the usual festivities despite the heat and on Boxing Day went off to Gauhati, where I met up with my friend Dilip Doshi. Dilip of course was on the staff at Trent Bridge in 1973 and 1974. A very talented slow left arm bowler, I remember him surprising Dickie Bird. The first time Bird umpired in a match involving Dilip, the Yorkshireman asked Dilip whether he should stand up to the wicket or allow Dilip to run between the wicket and the umpire. Dilip didn't bother to reply. He didn't have a run up. He simply stood and bowled. At least Dilip didn't use the tactic of John Steele who would suddenly emerge from behind the umpire and bowl—John Childs is another who is fond of this dodge. In his first seasons at Nottingham Dilip played very much the sort of role I imagine Ranjitsinhji and Duleepsinhji had performed in the distant past. He treated the staff at the cricket ground as his menials and this rather upset people like Frank Woodhead. In 1976 he had disappeared and was playing for one of the Minor Counties, but he came back to Trent Bridge the following year and during his second stint on the staff had a much better understanding of English ways. He and I used to spend hours in the nets playing mock Test Matches between England and India. Like me he went on to become a Test cricketer. His departure, the second time, from Trent Bridge was very sad and no doubt upset him. It occurred in 1978 when we signed Hadlee to replace Rice and then found it necessary to reinstate the South African, so unexpectedly landing ourselves with three overseas players, Dilip being the third. Dilip was strictly a bowler. His batting was of no account. Faced with the choice the Indian had to go. In the 1980s he had some good summers with Warwickshire.

The wicket at Gauhati was not up to county standard. Greig asked me to open the batting with Graham Barlow. We soon saw off the seam bowlers, then Doshi and a spinner with a very peculiar action, Bhattacharjee, took over. Fortunately I was well practised against Dilip, but he trapped Barlow leg before for 35. I made 55, the best score of the innings, before the mysterious Bhattacharjee clean bowled me. Bob Willis had the opposition—East Zone—in great difficulty; he took five for 29, but the game was drawn.

It was back to Calcutta for the Second Test. Despite my fifty at Gauhati, I felt that the captain was unlikely to change the winning team of the Delhi Test. Fate however decided otherwise. Keith Fletcher had twisted his ankle in a pothole outside the team's hotel and the ankle refused to respond immediately to treatment. This meant that there was an unexpected vacant batting place. In rungetting terms the choice was between myself and Roger Tolchard—or so I thought. The selectors thought otherwise, they included both of us and omitted Bob Woolmer.

Woolmer was unlucky. Leaving aside the fact that he was a native in these parts and apparently played his first cricket in

The obligatory tourist photo in India.

Calcutta, he had played a great part in the successes enjoyed by Kent during the 1970s. The first time I really remember him was in the Old Trafford Test the previous summer. I was 12th man. I suppose many of you readers will recall the famous game. Brian Close and John Edrich had the horrible task of trying to bat through the final eighty minutes of the third day, when England's final innings began in the late afternoon. Greig decided that Woolmer would go in if a wicket fell. Everyone, except Woolmer, retreated into the dressing room. Woolmer sat on the balcony as white as a sheet. He sat and he prayed. He was a very courageous bloke and I've no doubt would have gone over the top and held on if necessary. Fortunately for him no wicket fell.

When play ended, Close and Edrich returned. Close stared at me.

"Get me a drink, lad."

He took off his shirt and there were lumps sticking out of him where the ball had struck and bruises had swollen up. I've never seen anything quite like his battered body. I brought a tot of whisky.

"That's not a drink, lad. Fetch me a decent drink."

So I went away and returned with nearly half a pint.

There's a lovely picture somewhere of Close and Mushtaq both fielding at bat-pad. The batsman's gone to lap it. Mushtaq's jumping out of the way, Close is simply unmoved. Close was a tough leader. One of my early Sunday League games was against Somerset in the days when Close was skipper. Alan Jones misfielded a ball and Close threatened to send him off the field. I'm sure there would have been a bust up, if Merv Kitchen hadn't smoothed things over. Kitchen had played for Somerset and knew the best way to calm Close.

Back to my Test debut. The interesting feature of the two Test sides was the total contrast in the bowling. England had three seamers in Bob Willis, John Lever and Chris Old plus the captain who bowled both seam and spin and Derek Underwood as the only specialist spinner. India had three of the best spinners in the world, Bishen Bedi, Chandra and Prasanna, but their seam attack was of very modest proportions. Underwood was in fact unwell on the eve of the Test, but chosen just the same.

In the hour before play began I watched in horror as the groundsmen busily scrubbed every blade of grass off the pitch. It would suit their spinners in no time.

Bishen Bedi won the toss and elected to bat. The obvious choice, as scoring any runs in the final innings on that strip was going to be a miracle. India however made a terrible start. Chris Old took a tremendous catch off the third ball, bowled by Willis, to dismiss Gavaskar. It was a brilliant delivery and only someone of Gavaskar's skill could have got a bat to it.

Bob Willis was one of those bowlers who sent every ball 'down the corridor'. There was no doubt that at that time he was the best opening bowler in England. His first few seasons in first-class cricket had been difficult. At the time I started playing he had switched from Surrey to Warwickshire and from 1973 had established himself as a regular in the England team. A year or two later he was to be picked as England's captain. The selectors should never have given him that tricky job. Not because he lacked the expertise to be a captain, but because, as the main strike bowler, he needed to concentrate fully on bowling and to relax in between spells, rather than have the worry of rotating the bowling and placing the field.

My memory of that first day of Test cricket was of the enormous crowd and its accompanying noise of course, but as well, the way England fielded. No catches were dropped and the batsmen had to work hard to elude the fielders despite the fast outfield. After an hour or so there was an interval for much needed drinks and when lunch came India were 53 for two off 25 overs. Viswanath looked as if he had settled in, but Deadly Derek, who had recovered from his sick bed, had him caught at short-leg by Tolchard for 35. That score was to prove the best of the innings. At the close the total was 146 for seven off 69 overs.

The last three wickets added only nine runs on the second

day. We opened with Dennis Amiss and Graham Barlow. The idea of using Graham—he was normally first wicket down for Middlesex at this time—was that the Indian opening attack had so little talent that he could get his eye in before the spinners arrived. That was the theory (at least I think that was the theory), however Barlow's only scoring shot was a snick for four, then another snick off the inner edge went into the wicketkeeper's gloves. Mike Brearley, who had opened in the First Test, came to the crease. Bishen Bedi brought himself on and quickly sent Brearley packing, caught bat-pad. So I arrived with the score 14 for 2. Bedi increased the ring of close fieldsmen round the bat, the policy being to intimidate a novice. I felt I had to play my natural game and quickly late cut one to the boundary, then swept another for four. At lunch we had moved on to 37 for two. Amiss had batted for 17 overs for just eight. He was content to survive. After the interval I continued until I had made over 30, then got bogged down by Prasanna. I suppose eventually the slow scoring got to me and I tried something more adventurous, misjudged the spin and was out leg before. At the close on the second day we were 136 for four, Greig and Tolchard the not out batsmen. The third day was at once the most boring and the most courageous day's cricket I can remember. Tony Greig was taken ill overnight and there was some doubt whether he would be fit to reach the ground for the start of play. Somehow Greig not only staggered to the crease but batted right through the entire day scoring just 75 runs—149 were scored for the loss of two wickets, Tolchard and Knott.

Roger Tolchard 'Tolly' was a very similar player to Alan Knott, but he lacked Knott's flair behind the stumps. Playing at Grace Road, where Ray Illingworth liked wickets designed for off spin, Tolly became an expert at batting on a turning wicket. This helped him a great deal in India and his average was something above 40. In the Test Tolchard reached 67 before he was rather unlucky to be out. He played a ball on to his boot and from there it bounced to the wicket.

Some idea of the enormous crowds who watched us in India.

A rest day followed. Greig was 94 not out, but had made little effort to reach three figures before the close. He spent the day in bed. On the fourth day he quickly added the six runs he needed and then was leg before to Prasanna ... Old hit out, as wickets fell, and topped fifty. England's innings ended at 321.

I love fielding cover point to Chris Old. He positioned the fielder at cover with precision, the exact spot depending on the amount of swing he was getting on the ball. Most bowlers let the fielder find his own spot, but Old could gauge where the batsman would hit the ball and very often he was right. In a day in the field, while he was bowling, I might have to fetch one, or at most two, balls from the boundary rope. Like Mike Hendrick he sent down very few half volleys and therefore offered very little for the batsman to hit.

The pitch was now taking more spin, so, as India began their second innings, Greig's policy was to have Underwood bowling continuously at one end and use the seam bowlers in relays at the other, in fact he also put himself on, bowling his slow stuff.

Gavaskar started sketchily against Willis, but survived. Just before lunch Greig brought himself on—Underwood was already bowling at the Maidan end—and Gavaskar unaccountably played a wild shot to mid off, where Amiss dropped a sitter. It was not to be an expensive error, since soon after play resumed Underwood's faster ball deceived him and Gavaskar played on. Predictably Indian wickets fell with regularity and at stumps the score was 145 for seven. 21 needed to avoid an innings defeat.

The pitch was totally brown and the surface like powder. Anyone could see that the final day's play would not last long, yet about 65,000 spectators turned up, paying some exorbitant price for a ticket. Tickets for every day's play were at a premium. It was the practice of the England squad, who had an allocation of free tickets and did not need them, to go out and sell to the highest bidder. As I seemed to get on better with the spectators than most of the tourists, I found I inherited the job of hawking match tickets. The money earned went into the pot and was divided

The Christmas festivities away from home.

between us, which was fair enough, but what I didn't realise then was that the Indians were paying me anything up to a month's wages for these tickets. Looking back I feel ashamed that I was involved in this dubious trade, but no one thought anything of it in 1977.

Prasanna, one of the overnight batsmen, lasted less than two overs on the fifth morning, being caught in the slips off Underwood. Patel, the other not out batsman, was joined by the skipper, Bedi. Between them, much to the appreciation of the crowd—you'd have thought the match had been won to judge by the applause—the two saved an innings defeat.

Amiss and Barlow needed 16 runs to win. Barlow looked very uncomfortable, he had failed in three successive Test innings; he couldn't afford to be out this time. Luckily for him he was dropped in the slips. We won by ten wickets.

The Calcutta crowd seemed to blame the selectors rather than the players for the defeat. The selectors were hissed and booed and a shower of oranges and banana peel rained down on them when they walked into the pavilion.

England were two up in the five match series. The third game was in Madras, a much more leisurely place than Calcutta and much cleaner. Keith Fletcher had still not fully recovered from his ankle injury, so the single change in our side was the inclusion of Bob Woolmer for Barlow. The match was dominated by the 'Vaseline Incident', which I feel was making a mountain out of a molehill. John Lever was accused of shining the ball by using the Vaseline he had on his eyebrows designed to prevent sweat running into his eyes. Bedi made some rather pointed comments, but Greig was very diplomatic and didn't rise to the bait. The spectators managed some large banners, some more odd than others, and one I recall read:

"True with Vaseline, ball keeps its shine,
Lever, bowl true, if you have spine."

We won the game, and therefore the series, decisively. My contribution was almost entirely in the field, since in the first

Receiving the Man of the Match award in Indore.

innings, I managed to run myself out for 2—Brearley and I hesitated over a second run—and in the second, I had only just got to the crease when I tried to cut a ball from Chandra. It got up higher than I anticipated and the wicketkeeper took the catch.

India had some consolation when they won the Fourth Test, whilst the Fifth was a very exciting draw. We required 214 to win in about four hours and were 152 for seven when play ended—Keith Fletcher at last had a chance to show his true worth and was 58 not out. I made 15 and 22.

I will close this piece with two comments which were written in the essay on the tour published in 'Wisden':

"Randall made his Test debut in the electric and awe-inspiring atmosphere of Calcutta's Eden Gardens. He came in with England in trouble on a pitch of dubious quality. He proceeded to make 37 with an assurance not equalled hitherto by another English batsman. Obviously he had the technique to build a major Test innings, but finished the series without improving on his maiden effort."

"Undoubtedly the main factor in England's superiority was the bowling, supported by fielding of a standard that has not been touched recently, if ever, by English Test sides."

Those two quotes made by Dicky Rutnagar are a suitable note on which to end my first overseas Test tour to India.

INDIA v ENGLAND

Played at Eden Gardens, Calcutta, January 1, 2, 3, 5, 6, 1977
England won by ten wickets.

INDIA

1	S.M. Gavaskar	c Old b Willis	0	b Underwood	18
2	A.D. Gaekwad	b Lever	32	c Tolchard b Greig	8
3	P. Sharma	c Greig b Lever	9	c Knott b Willis	20
4	G.R. Viswanath	c Tolchard b Underwood	35	c Lever b Greig	3
5	B.P. Patel	hit wkt b Willis	21	lbw b Old	56
6	E.D. Solkar	c Greig b Willis	2	c Knott b Willis	3
7	S. Madan Lal	c Knott b Old	17	c Brearley b Old	16
8	+S.M.H. Kirmani	not out	25	b Old	0
9	E.A.S. Prasanna	b Willis	2	c Brearley b Underwood	13
10	*B.S. Bedi	c Lever b Old	1	b Underwood	18
11	B.S. Chandrasekhar	b Willis	1	not out	4
	Extras	lb 2, nb 8	10	b 2, lb 4, nb 16	22
	Total		155		181

1-1 2-23 3-65 4-92 5-99 6-106 7-136 8-147 9-149

1-31 2-33 3-36 4-60 5-70 6-97 7-97 8-146 9-171

Bowling	O	M	R	W	O	M	R	W
Willis	20	3	27	5	13	1	32	2
Lever	22	2	57	2	3	0	12	0
Underwood	13	5	24	1	32.5	18	50	3
Old	20	5	37	2	12	4	38	3
Greig					10	0	27	2

ENGLAND

1	D.L. Amiss	c Kirmani b Prasanna	35	not out	7
2	G.D. Barlow	c Kirmani b Madan Lal	4	not out	7
3	J.M. Brearley	c Solkar b Bedi	5		
4	D.W. Randall	lbw b Prasanna	37		
5	R.W. Tolchard	b Bedi	67		
6	*A.W. Greig	lbw b Prasanna	103		
7	+A.P.E. Knott	c Gavaskar b Bedi	2		
8	C.M. Old	c Madan Lal b Prasanna	52		
9	J.K. Lever	c Gavaskar b Bedi	2		
10	D.L. Underwood	c Gavaskar b Bedi	4		
11	R.G.D. Willis	not out	0		
	Extras	b 5, lb 5	10	lb 1, nb 1	2
	Total		321	(0 wkt)	16

1-7 2-14 3-81 4-90 5-232 6-234 7-298 8-307 9-321

Bowling	O	M	R	W	O	M	R	W
Madan Lal	17	4	25	1	1	0	3	0
Solkar	6	1	15	0				
Bedi	64	25	110	5	1.4	0	6	0
Chandrasekhar	33	9	66	0				
Prasanna	57.4	16	93	4	1	0	5	0
Sharma	1	0	2	0				

Umpires: B. Satyaji Rao and H.P. Sharma

Toss: India

Close of Play: 1st day: India 146-7 (Kirmani 20*, Prasanna 1*); 2nd day: England 136-4 (Tolchard 31*, Greig 19*); 3rd day: England 285-6 (Greig 94*, Old 35*), 4th day: India(2) 145-7 (Patel 48*, Prasanna 12*).

CHAPTER 7

Celebrating a Centenary

I was eleven years old when I went to my first great cricket match. Dad had a day off and we caught the bus in The Square, destination Worksop. The bus drops you off almost next to the cricket ground, though the ground itself, hidden behind rows of terraced Victorian houses, is not really visible until you walk down a short street, and over a bridge spanning the river, which is little more than a large stream. Notts were playing Yorkshire. The sensible place to sit is on the embankment, across from the entrance, but I wanted to be part of the action and dragged Dad to a spot as near to the boundary line as possible. We put our macs on the grass and sat down. I don't believe I moved all day—I did at the end to stand in a queue waiting for Freddie Trueman's autograph. What do I remember of the cricket? The bowling of Trueman and a six hit out of the ground by John Springall.

There was however one aspect I didn't understand. Here was a vast throng of spectators (in fact probably about two thousand, but the largest crowd I'd seen) and the cricketers ignored them. Dad and I sat on the grass with, for much of the day, a fielder standing two or three yards away—the boundaries at Worksop are not over long—and throughout those six hours, the fielder, or two or three different fielders would pretend we weren't present at all. Changing positions between overs they'd walk towards us eyes on the grass by their feet. When a wicket fell, they'd stand, hands in pockets, as if they were alone. At the time this attitude struck me as not very polite—rude is perhaps too strong a word.

This thought lodged in the back of my mind. It didn't occur to me then that I was in fact paying that impolite man to entertain me, and a poor job he was making of it, but ten years later, when I was lucky enough to be paid to entertain people by playing cricket, I determined that that was what I would do.

In my first year or two at Trent Bridge my being was entirely taken up with the task of winning a place in the county side and the next seasons by simply making sure I kept my place.

My trip to India was the greatest experience of my life and for the two months of that tour the pressures to retain a place in the side were to an extent relaxed; I could be myself. So far as amusing the crowd when fielding was concerned, the matches gave an ideal opportunity at two levels. My comic gestures and mimes suited the Indian audience to a tee and secondly the over rates were so painfully slow that they allowed ample opportunity to perform a cartwheel, do a somersault, play tricks with my sunhat, wink at a pretty girl.

So when we flew to Australia, after a brief visit to Sri Lanka, I was happy. I was relaxed. Even the hours of delay stuck in airport lounges didn't unduly worry me.

Before the Centenary Test in Melbourne, a three day game had been arranged in Perth. Most of the press had written England off so far as winning the Test was concerned. It was pointed out that the England team had been picked to suit conditions in India. The Test series in India had been won and the victors were exhausted by their efforts and longed to go home. Australia regarded themselves as the world champions and had just completed an easy win over New Zealand. The previous season they had beaten West Indies 5 to 1.

The final batting place in our side for the Test rested between myself and Graham Barlow. Graham batted better in the game at

Perth, but the selectors decided to stick with me, Bob Woolmer came in for Tolchard compared with the team for the Fifth Test in India. The other alteration was simply that Chris Old, who had missed the last Test due to back trouble, returned, replacing Mike Selvey, his stand-in.

Some idea of the way the Australians regarded the match prior to the start can be gauged by the sarcastic comment made when it was announced that the fifth day would be used up with a 40 overs game if the match finished early. The comment was, "What will the players do on the fourth day?"

Dennis Lillee was the dominant figure in the Australian side. I'd never batted against him before. The Australians had played Notts in 1972, but I wasn't in the county side. In 1975 they didn't meet the county and didn't play at Trent Bridge either in the World Cup or in the Test series. I knew him therefore by reputation only, but in the brief particulars of the players in the Test Match programme, it simply said:

"Generally regarded as the best bowler of his type in the world."

It might be worthwhile just reprinting the short paragraph which described me in 'World of Cricket' on the eve of the game:

"Derek Randall of Notts is another young, likeable lad, a middle order batsman and a brilliant, explosive cover fielder. He prowls about the covers and with his continuous moving about, makes it difficult for the batsman to place him. He is extremely quick over a few yards and pops up like a jack-in-a-box where you least expect him. He has lots of ability as a wristy batsman and if enthusiasm got players to the top, he would be there already. He is a natural stroke player on all types of pitches and has a refreshing, uninhibited attitude to the game."

The atmosphere for the Centenary Test was that of a great jamboree. All the old Test cricketers had arrived to view the game. The Queen and Duke of Edinburgh were scheduled to visit the ground on the last day of the match and in addition the game had been organised to coincide with Melbourne's 'Moomba Week'.

Dennis Lillee being chaired from the field after Australia's victory.

THE 'D' STANDS FOR DESTROYER

AUSTRALIA retained its world champion crown with a historic Centenary Test win over England at the MCG yesterday, and the 45-run victory an hour before stumps was a repeat result of the first official Test between the two countries at the same ground in 1877.

At one stage England was in a strong position to snatch an incredible win, but it faltered after tea when the Australian attack swept through the lower order England batsmen.

Once again the destroyer was Dennis Lillee, who took five wickets. Lillee, who is unavailable for the English tour because of a back injury, was chaired from the field, and was awarded a special trophy for the best bowling performance in the Test.

The $1500 sponsor's prize for the Man of the Match went to England's Derek Randall, who was out yesterday for a magnificent 174 in his first Test against Australia, a score which nearly enabled England to pull of a stunning upset.

England was all out for 417, a record for an England fourth innings.

PICTURE: The destroyer, Dennis Lillee, walks off the MCG at the break for lunch yesterday.

Greig won the toss for England—a specially-minted gold coin was used for the job. He took a gamble and decided to field. The pitch had moisture in it and he felt that Lillee would destroy us. Neither of the openers survived long. Ian Davis played across the line to a ball from John Lever and was trapped leg before. His opening partner, Ric McCosker, was very unlucky. A ball from Bob Willis hit his hand and shot straight up to his jaw, then down on to his wicket. It was then found that his jaw had been fractured in the process.

Our bowling and fielding matched the standard we had reached in India. The Australians came and went. Only the captain, Greg Chappell, had any real answer. He batted about four hours and made just 40. Rodney Marsh lashed out with two brilliant boundaries, but perished shortly afterwards.

Willis, Lever, Old and Underwood shared the wickets between them and Australia were bowled out for 138. The press had a field day. It was reckoned the worst day Australia had had since The Ashes began. Tony Greig said: "If I live to be 95 I shall never forget this day." A most unfortunate number to pick, as it turned out!

Greig decided to open the innings with Woolmer and Mike Brearley, dropping Dennis Amiss down the order. There was less than an hour's play left on the first day when the English innings began. Lillee removed Woolmer; Underwood went in as nightwatchman and batted out time.

"England's rosy dreams of a brilliant success in the prestigious Melbourne Centenary Test were transformed into an agonising nightmare yesterday," ran the opening sentence of the report of the second day's play. Before the umpires sent the teams in for lunch, we had lost seven more wickets. Lillee and the local hero, Max Walker, had taken now four wickets each.

Mike Brearley was caught at third slip by David Hookes off Lillee's out-swinger in the first over. He had not added to his overnight score of 12. I came in, but in the second over—from Walker—Underwood was out. Lillee had me ducking to a bouncer

A handstand whilst captain Greig relaxes.

and I cheekily doffed my cap. He smiled but put on even more pace and the second of two short pitched deliveries flew off my bat to Marsh behind the stumps. Dennis Amiss was no more fortunate; he was dropped by Marsh, off Lillee, but at the other end submitted to Walker, driving the ball into the hands of O'Keeffe. Keith Fletcher lasted no longer, another catch to Rod Marsh.

Tony Greig thought the only way out was to hit. Off 20 balls he reached 18.The crowd was chanting Lill-ee, Lill-ee, Lill-ee. It was Walker however who bowled Greig off his pads. Knott managed double figures, but Lillee soon disposed of the tail-enders. If the first day had been a terrible one for Australia, today they had their revenge.

Half the day's play still remained. The pundits blamed Greig for changing the batting order, replacing Amiss with Woolmer, but on the day I doubt if it would have made much difference.

Ian Davis proved that it was possible to bat on the wicket. He had scored a hundred earlier that season in a Test against Pakistan and he now showed that he was a very competent opening batsman. By the close of play he was 45 not out, alternating between great care and some nice square cuts. Chappell took the unusual step of making Kerry O'Keeffe, the leg spinner, Davis's opening partner. The ploy worked and O'Keeffe made a very sensible 14 runs. The steady opening partnership, worth 33, calmed the hysteria. Chris Old captured the prize wicket of Greg Chappell, bowled between bat and pad; Cosier mistimed a hook and Australia were 53 for three, 96 ahead. Another wicket that second evening would at least bring us some hope. Doug Walters came in ahead of the inexperienced David Hookes. Walters was dropped by Bob Willis and the scoreboard showed Australia 104 for three when we went back to the hotel for the night.

I can't remember many matches where the press swayed so violently from praise to abuse from one day to the next. By the close of the third day, the journalists described us as 'the mugs of

Australia and martyrs thrown to the lions'. The team selection came in for increasing criticism—why were Geoff Miller and Graham Barlow left out?

The reason for this criticism was the batting of Australia in their second innings. The score rose to 387 for eight. One reporter excelled himself blaming this total on 'the domestic policy of insular selfishness by the counties', whatever that meant.

The fact was that the pitch eased. The overnight pair of Davis and Walters took the score to 132, when Davis's careful innings ended. Doug Walters made a good 66 before being caught off Greig by Alan Knott. Hookes was fortunate not to touch two deliveries from Greig, but not long afterwards hit five balls in succession to the boundary off the captain. Marsh and Lillee added 76 for the eighth wicket, with Marsh looking very sound. When Lillee went, to our amazement Ric McCosker re-appeared, his jaw wired up and head swathed in bandages. Australia were almost 400 ahead by this time and it seemed completely unnecessary to ask McCosker to bat. I was glad I wasn't a fast bowler. Lever chanced one or two bouncers, but his heart didn't seem to be in them. Marsh and McCosker were still there, not out 95 and 17, when play ended.

We had a day off. The main question was whether the game would last into the fifth; some of the pessimists of the pre-match days were re-emerging. When play resumed, Rod Marsh duly scored the five he needed for a hundred—it was the first time an Australian wicketkeeper had scored a century against England, and he didn't give a single chance.

Tony Greig, despite the critics, kept to Woolmer and Brearley as our opening pair in the second innings. They seemed to be coping well until the last over before lunch, when Woolmer was leg before to Walker. My innings began directly after the forty minute break. In the two hours between lunch and tea, Mike Brearley and I placed Australia on the defensive for the first time. I managed to time a couple of hook shots off Lillee's bouncers and found few problems with the spin of Gilmour and O'Keeffe.

Lillee broke our partnership directly after tea, when Brearley was lbw. No other wicket fell although the light became increasingly difficult—play ended 18 minutes early because of it. Dennis Amiss had acquired the reputation of being Lillee's rabbit. He was clearly nervous when he arrived to fill Brearley's place, but slowly grew in confidence and by the time play ended we were 191 for two.

England required 272 to win on the final day. In theory it was possible, but England had never reached 463 in the fourth innings of a Test before, so the experts said.

Dennis Amiss and I added 46 off 13 overs before Lillee returned with the new ball. This was going to be the crucial part of the innings. The first delivery with the new ball produced a loud appeal by Lillee for a catch behind the wicket. He glared at me and said something, but I was not going to be brow-beaten and replied in like vein. I tried to ignore the short pitched stuff as much as possible. Walker and Lillee grew tired. Lillee bowled off a shorter run and was less dangerous. The Australian attack, with Gilmour very inaccurate, was weakening. Greg Chappell brought himself on and in his second over got one to keep low and cut back; Amiss was confused and bowled. We had put on 166 in something under 4 hours. Keith Fletcher came, made a single and was caught by Marsh.

Tony Greig arrived. He hit Lillee for two excellent fours and gave the impression that England were marching to victory. I became a little over-confident and, backing up too far, nearly ran myself out—the fielder's throw missed the stumps. I had to thank Rod Marsh, so often thought of as the hard man in Australian cricket, for my next escape. The umpire gave me out caught by Marsh when I had made 161. I walked, but Marsh called me back, saying that the ball hadn't carried. Considering the vital stage the match was in at that point, it was a very fine gesture on Marsh's part.

Greg Chappell is a very careful bowler; he keeps a tidy line and length. Both Greig and myself found it very difficult to score

The 1976-77 'touring team in Bombay.

off him. His afternoon spell of ten overs for 13 runs tells its own story.

Chappell brought O'Keeffe back into the attack. I pushed forward to a leg break and sent the ball to Cosier in the leg trap. My innings was at an end. I wandered, rather dazed by the applause, towards the pavilion, through the gate and slap into the Queen and Duke of Edinburgh, who had arrived on the ground a few minutes earlier: it was the wrong gate. The Queen was amused, I was embarrassed and retreated to the right exit.

I had scored 174 and our total was 346 for five. There still seemed to be a chance. The tail was not too strong, but Greig and Knott were both capable batsmen. The tea interval was taken up by the teams being presented to the Queen. We required 117 in 130 minutes. However Tony Greig was dismissed in an identical fashion to myself. Chris Old hit out wildly and was caught; Lever went leg before to a googly and with just under an hour's play left, our last hope, Alan Knott, was leg before to Lillee for 42. Lillee who had taken eleven wickets in the match was lifted shoulder high and carried out the field. Australia had won by 45 runs: exactly the same result as the very first Test.

The crowd seemed rather reluctant to go home. They watched the usual presentation ceremony with more interest than normal. I received the Man of the Match award and 1,500 Australian dollars.

I couldn't have asked for a better finale to my first tour with England. I had been away from home for four months and once away from the ground and in the hotel, my thoughts were mainly to get home and put my feet up. We had a great reception when we landed at Heathrow—the plane not only carried the England team, but also many of the old England cricketers who had travelled out to watch the match. Ken Barrington spoke to the press on our arrival in London and described the tour as the best he had been on.

There was less than a fortnight to go before the English season started. The Mayor of Retford had organised a lunch in my

Showing my Centenary Test bat to Joe Hardstaff and Bill Voce.

honour in the Town Hall and quite a crowd gathered to greet my return to the town. Another reception was set up by the County Council and with one thing and another it was soon time to report back to Trent Bridge.

Although it was not yet public knowledge, behind the scenes Kerry Packer, with the help of Tony Greig, on the English front, was setting up his World Series Cricket in rivalry to the Australian Board. I was asked to join the 'Circus', but aside from the ethics of the matter, I had just won a place in the England team and was anxious to hold it. Initially, apart from Tony Greig, Alan Knott, John Snow and Derek Underwood signed up. Dennis Amiss and Bob Woolmer also joined Packer.

The whole business became public about the time the Australian touring party came to England. It turned out that virtually all the tourists had moved into the Packer camp. Most of the leading West Indians also joined.

I shall finish this chapter with some brief notes on the 1977 series against Australia. I suppose uppermost in my mind must always remain my first Test at Trent Bridge, when Geoff Boycott ran me out. A form of rough justice considering the times that I was responsible for either myself or my partner getting out.

I think Clive Rice lost most of his hair on the day, I believe it was a Middlesex match at Lord's, when I ran out three men. The middle of the three was Bruce French and I don't think I can be blamed for his dismissal. I was running to the danger end. John Emburey's powerful throw however missed one set of stumps and the ball flew past Bruce knocking down the wicket at his end.

I made about 60 and was not looking forward to greeting Rice in the dressing room.

"I'm batting like Wally Hammond, but running like Charlie Chaplin." I said as I opened the door. Clive hadn't a ready answer to that!

The one run out that upset me most was in New Zealand. I had flown over especially for a match for Richard Hadlee's benefit. I had better say, here, that I admit to the habit of playing the ball and immediately looking as if I am about to run, whether I intend to, or not. Hadlee decided I should open the batting with a young lad, for whom this was clearly the most important occasion of his cricketing life. I took strike and ran him out first ball. I still blush when I recall the incident.

My reputation over the years for run outs has built up to the stage where I am normally the scapegoat for any Notts run out. In fact someone had the nerve to blame me last summer for a run out, when I wasn't even batting. I wasn't happy, to which he responded:

"Well if you had been batting, it would have been you!"

The 1977 series was Geoff Boycott's return to Test cricket after his self-imposed exile and he really dominated the last three Tests, making his hundredth 100 in the game at Headingley. The other landmark was the Test debut of Ian Botham. We won the One Day Internationals two games to one and the Tests three matches to nil.

My best performance for England was in the Second Test at Old Trafford. Manchester's the place where invariably some wag in a cloth cap will say, as you leave the pavilion:

"Don't shut gate, lad, you'll soon be back."

And when you are back in a minute, it makes you feel dreadful. Luckily I scored 79 in that Test, and, as England won by nine wickets, didn't bat a second time.

AUSTRALIA v ENGLAND

Played at Melbourne, March 12, 13, 14, 16, 17, 1977
Australia won by 45 runs.

AUSTRALIA

1	I.C. Davis	lbw b Lever	5	c Knott b Greig	68
2	R.B. McCosker	b Willis	4	(10) c Greig b Old	25
3	G.J. Cosier	c Fletcher b Lever	10	(4) c Knott b Lever	4
4	*G.S. Chappell	b Underwood	40	(3) b Old	2
5	D.W. Hookes	c Greig b Old	17	(6) c Fletcher b Underwood	56
6	K.D. Walters	c Greig b Willis	4	(5) c Knott b Greig	66
7	+R.W. Marsh	c Knott b Old	28	not out	110
8	G.J. Gilmour	c Greig b Old	4	b Lever	16
9	K.J. O'Keeffe	c Brearley b Underwood	0	(2) c Willis b Old	14
10	D.K. Lillee	not out	10	(9) c Amiss b Old	25
11	M.H.N. Walker	b Underwood	2	not out	8
	Extras	b 4, lb 2, nb 8	14	lb 10, nb 15	25
Total			138	(9 wkts dec)	419

1-11 2-13 3-23 4-45 5-51 6-102 7-114 8-117 9-136

1-33 2-40 3-53 4-132 5-187 6-244 7-277 8-353 9-407

Bowling	O	M	R	W	O	M	R	W
Lever	12	1	36	2	21	1	95	2
Willis	8	0	33	2	22	0	91	0
Old	12	4	39	3	27.6	2	104	4
Underwood	11.6	2	16	3	12	2	38	1
Greig					14	5	66	2

ENGLAND

1	R.A. Woolmer	c Chappell b Lillee	9	lbw b Walker	12
2	J.M. Brearley	c Hookes b Lillee	12	lbw b Lillee	43
3	D.L. Underwood	c Chappell b Walker	7	(10) b Lillee	7
4	D.W. Randall	c Marsh b Lillee	4	(3) c Cosier b O'Keeffe	174
5	D.L. Amiss	c O'Keeffe b Walker	4	(4) b Chappell	64
6	K.W.R. Fletcher	c Marsh b Walker	4	(5) c Marsh b Lillee	1
7	*A.W. Greig	b Walker	18	(6) c Cosier b O'Keeffe	41
8	+A.P.E. Knott	lbw b Lillee	15	(7) lbw b Lillee	42
9	C.M. Old	c Marsh b Lillee	3	(8) c Chappell b Lillee	2
10	J.K. Lever	c Marsh b Lillee	11	(9) lbw b O'Keeffe	4
11	R.G.D. Willis	not out	1	not out	5
	Extras	b 2, lb 2, w 1, nb 2	7	b 8, lb 4, w 3, nb 7	22
Total			95		417

1-19 2-30 3-34 4-40 5-40 6-61 7-65 8-78 9-86

1-28 2-113 3-279 4-290 5-346 6-369 7-380 8-385 9-410

Bowling	O	M	R	W	O	M	R	W
Lillee	13.3	2	26	6	34.4	7	139	5
Walker	15	3	54	4	22	4	83	1
O'Keeffe	1	0	4	0	33	6	108	3
Gilmour	5	3	4	0	4	0	29	0
Chappell					16	7	29	1
Walters					3	2	7	0

Umpires: T.F. Brooks and M.G.O'Connell

Toss: England

Close of Play: 1st day: England 29-1 (Brearley 12*, Underwood 5*); 2nd day: Australia(2) 104-3 (Davis 45*, Walters 32*); 3rd day: Australia(2) 387-8 (Marsh 95*, McCosker 17*), 4th day: England(2) 191-2 (Randall 87*, Amiss 34*).

CHAPTER 8

An Astonishing Recovery

Mike Brearley addresses me as, "Twasack". A word which he claims to be a nice swear word. A description which he also believes applies to my cricket.

Brearley took over the England captaincy, when Greig was forced to resign, having signed for Packer. There is general agreement that he was the most intelligent county captain of his time—Gatting had an unenviable task when he took over the Middlesex leadership from Brearley. I found that Brearley understood me better than other captains and we became good friends. Once or twice he stayed with us at Cropwell Butler, when Middlesex were playing at Trent Bridge. The visit I particularly recall was in June 1981. The match provides an excellent example of how Brearley's leadership could win matches.

Clive Rice won the toss, put Middlesex in and Hadlee aided by Rice, Cooper and Hemmings rolled them over. They were all out for 151 in 43.3 overs. They owed that modest total to Roland Butcher and Mike Selvey who between them made 113. No one else reached double figures. When we batted eight of our team made 20 or more. The only person to fail was myself. Typical of me, I'd made 162 not out against the Lancashire attack, then I failed to score a single run. The second ball I faced, bowled by

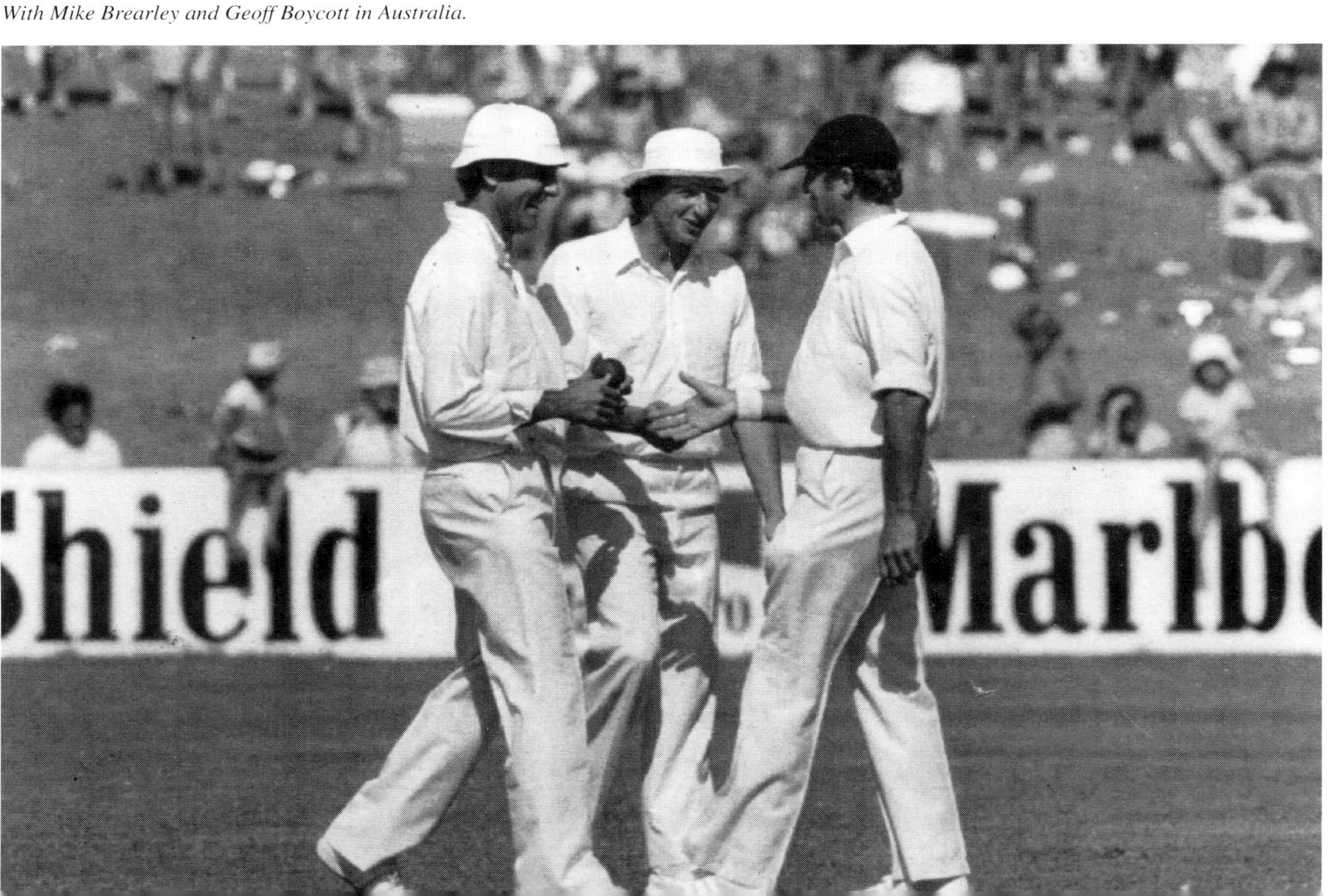

With Mike Brearley and Geoff Boycott in Australia.

Simon Hughes, I hooked and was caught by Phil Edmonds.

That evening as we had supper, Mike smiled when I complained that he knew all my weak points and had Edmonds stationed in just the right spot. He then said that he would get me out the same way in the second innings. The match was in a very interesting state. We had gained a first innings lead of 158. Middlesex in their second innings, which began before lunch on the second day, fell to 16 for two at the interval, with Barlow and Radley both dismissed by Hadlee. Soon after lunch, Gatting was caught by Basher Hassan off Eddie Hemmings—49 for three. It looked all over. Brearley however was still in. Roland Butcher hit out very effectively, making fifty in as many minutes. By the close Middlesex were 283 for four, Brearley not out 89 and Edmonds not out 87. It was at this point that Brearley made his comment.

We eventually got rid of Brearley for 131. He had batted almost exactly a day—from half past twelve on Monday to half past twelve on Tuesday. Anyway we had three and half hours to make 239. Paul Todd was leg before to Simon Hughes for three in the sixth over. I came in. Hughes's first ball to me was a no ball. Second ball came up nicely just right for the hook. I'd checked when I came in that no fielder was in place for the hook. I hooked, my eye followed the path of the ball; I began to run, then I saw Clive Radley, a yard in from the boundary waiting for the ball to descend. I looked at Brearley and I departed, even before the ball was in Radley's hands. Foiled again!

Brearley brought on his spinners, Emburey and Edmonds and the rest of the Notts batsmen, including Rice and Hadlee, formed a procession between the pitch and the dressing room. We were all out for 126. There was a minor row at the end because Hemmings had been injured and five minutes' "injury time" was added. The last wicket fell in this "injury time", but Brearley thoroughly deserved his victory.

My first tour under Mike Brearley's captaincy was to Pakistan and New Zealand in the winter following the Centenary Test. Having enjoyed touring India and especially the response

I got from the spectators, I was looking forward to returning to the Indian sub-continent. I must say that I was disappointed with this second visit. I'm not one who knows much about history and politics, but there is little doubt that the atmosphere in Pakistan at the time was not very pleasant. So far as the cricket itself was concerned, the wickets were dead and as a result, all three Tests were drawn. In the midst of these problems came the rather farcical situation with the Pakistan Test players, who had signed for Packer. Mushtaq Mohammad, Imran Khan and Zaheer were undoubtedly Pakistan's best cricketers. After the First Test at Lahore, where little more than the first innings of each team was completed, conflicting announcements arrived at frequent intervals as to whether or not Pakistan would reinforce their team with the Packer men. We discussed the problem and debated whether we should refuse to play if Mushtaq and his colleagues took the field. In the end they didn't and the matter blew over.

I must say that I was pleased when the Pakistan leg of the tour was completed and we were flying to New Zealand. A few days before we left however Mike Brearley had his left arm broken batting in a minor game in Karachi. Thus we went off to New Zealand under a very different style of leadership—that of Geoff Boycott.

Graham Roope and Brian Rose were two of the cricketers who had not been on the 1976/77 tour. Roope could catch fresh air. I have never seen such a brilliant slip field as he was. Willis, Lever and Hendrick cheered up immediately when they saw Graham standing in the slips. However he hated the conditions in Pakistan and every day would report to anyone who would listen, how much more weight he'd lost. He measured his weight by the band round his wrist and reckoned it went round twice by the time we left Pakistan.

I can picture Brian Rose now, sitting in the lounge of our hotel reading some highbrow paper and smoking a cigar. He was very quiet, very thoughtful. Not an outgoing type of bloke at all and a bit too serious for me. He played some good Test innings, but like so many came unstuck against the West Indies.

It was the first time I'd been on tour with Bob Taylor. Alan Knott having signed up for Packer, the selectors chose Bob as our leading wicketkeeper with Paul Downton as the stand in: Tolchard, who'd been number two last year, was ignored.

If you've got any problems, Bob's the person to sort them out. He's also very good at the never-ending stream of functions which become part of everyday living for the touring cricketer. They're not really my cup of tea, but Bob will chat to anyone about anything. A very sociable man altogether.

My batting average in Pakistan was not of great note and during the New Zealand leg of the tour, Geoff Boycott decided to see if he could change my batting style—my average dropped from 26 to 11, I will say no more.

I don't wish to dwell too closely on the New Zealand leg of the tour. We played three Tests, the first of which was lost. It was the first time New Zealand had ever beaten England. We won the second game and the vital deciding third match was drawn despite being allotted six days. I recall the catch I took in the covers to remove Burgess, the New Zealand captain, but in contrast to our fielding in the second Test—which really won that game—suddenly catches were being dropped and New Zealand built up a good first innings total. John Lever who rarely makes a mistake in the outfield missed Geoff Howarth and the wicketkeeper, Edwards, and both made substantial scores. I opened the batting with Geoff Boycott and we started confidently, putting 30 on in seven overs before the close of play on the second day. On the third day everyone got bogged down and it soon became evident that despite the six days the match would be drawn.

Before I leave this tour, the run out incident at Christchurch has come to mind. I came in first wicket down when Brian Rose was caught off Collinge. Boycott was batting at the other end and we'd put on about 20. Ewen Chatfield ran up to bowl to Boycott. I watched him approaching the wicket and moved a few inches out of my crease; Chatfield stopped dead and knocked off one of the bails. The spectators were, if anything more disgusted than myself. It was the most uncricketlike action I can recall in any first-class game in which I've taken part. I think Mark Burgess put Chatfield up to it. I'm pleased to say that Ewen Chatfield and I soon forgot the incident and are the best of friends today.

I have to admit that I didn't have a brilliant tour—I thought I might just have a quick glance at Geoff Boycott's book which came out in 1980, to see what comments he made, if any, about me, particularly my batting. There is a single chapter in which he describes well-known players he's played with or against. The piece on myself I will give in its entirety:

"You can't write about the best players in the game without including Derek Randall for his fielding alone. His strength is his ability to anticipate where the batsman intends to seek a single. He challenges you to match your pace against his reactions and he is amazingly quick off the mark. His exuberance on the field makes him especially dangerous because it is difficult to pinpoint his position. I always study field placings and try to memorise them before I face a delivery but with Randall there is never any certainty that he will be where you expect him. He stands deep but as the bowler runs in he walks forward, skips, jogs a pace or two ... and by the time you play a stroke he is fifteen yards closer than you remember and closing fast. Very disconcerting. Randall saves runs on his reputation because batsmen are increasingly unwilling to take him on and he likes to play on that. He will challenge a batsman to run, amble towards the ball, smiling and beckoning him to risk it. Yet his concentration never wavers. Even when he's playing to the crowd—flicking the ball to hand with his heel, dropping his cap and flicking on to his head—he is always aware of the batsman's position, the possibilities of the situation. He can clown yet concentrate, even amid the pressure of a Test Match, and that is a gift I hope he never loses."

I can do no more than thank Geoff for the compliments which he pays to my fielding ability. The interesting omission in that description is any mention of me as a batsman. I suspect he gave up on me after that trip to New Zealand!

The England selectors did just that as well. Pakistan and New Zealand toured England in 1978. I was not invited to play in any of the six Test Matches. I'm not an expert on the records, but it is worthwhile just looking at the team which represented England in the first home Test in 1977 against that of twelve months later:

1977	1978
D.L. Amiss	B. Wood
J.M. Brearley	J.M. Brearley
R.A. Woolmer	C.T. Radley
D.W. Randall	D.I. Gower
A.W. Greig	G.R.J. Roope
G.D. Barlow	G. Miller
A.P.E. Knott	R.W. Taylor
C.M. Old	C.M. Old
J.K. Lever	I.T. Botham
D.L. Underwood	P.H. Edmonds
R.G.D. Willis	R.G.D. Willis

Only three of the 1977 team survived for 1978. Is it a record? I don't know. It's true that Amiss, Greig, Knott, Woolmer and Underwood were all Packer men, but even the absence of those five didn't prevent the selectors from ignoring myself, Barlow and Lever. I shouldn't criticise because England won two of the Tests v Pakistan and all three against New Zealand.

When the team was chosen to go to Australia in the winter of 1978/79, I found I had made enough runs for Nottinghamshire to grab the last batting place in the squad of sixteen. Could I actually get into the Test side, or would I be one of those unlucky individuals who mooned around with the reserve wicketkeeper, acting as twelfth man and doing other chores?

It was a bit more of a wrench to leave England compared with the first tour of 1976/77, because not only was I abandoning Liz, but also my young son, Simon, now a year and half old. Our team would also be in direct opposition, so far as entertaining the public was concerned, to Kerry Packer's Super-Tests.

The ball comes on to the bat much more quickly in Australia than in England and I hadn't been long away from home when I began to benefit from the difference. There were four first-class games before the First Test. I was not selected for the opening match in Adelaide, but played in the other three games, making 63 at Melbourne, 110 at Sydney and 66 and 47 at Brisbane. With England having two all-rounders in Botham and Miller, the final specialist batting place rested between myself and Clive Radley. Radley is a rather unnatural player, like me, I suppose. He's a groundsman's nightmare, wearing flat shoes and sliding to the crease when he completes a run. He was unlucky to have a run of poor scores at the start of the tour. Hit on the head by a ball from Rodney Hogg, this clearly unnerved him. As it turned out the Test side established itself in the first game of the series and nine of the eleven played in all six Tests, the only changes being to the bowlers, with Edmonds, Lever and Old playing once each.

If our side more or less selected itself, Australia were the opposite. The publicity experts in Packer's camp were doing all they could to divert attention away from our team to World Series Cricket, in which virtually all the well-known Australian players were appearing.

Graham Yallop led Australia. He had a very difficult task because so many of his team were playing together for the first time. The opening Test was staged at Brisbane. Brearley decided to play both our spinners, Edmonds and Miller, and left out Mike Hendrick, which meant we were without our best slip fielder. Yallop won the toss and decided to bat—a difficult decision because the atmosphere early on would help the swing. It was the first time I had played in a Test with David Gower. The Australian opening batsmen, Wood and Cosier, did not appreciate that with myself on one side of the wicket and David Gower on the other quick singles are not advised. The first wicket that fell therefore had nothing to do with atmosphere and swing, but all to do with

Gower swooping on the ball and flicking it to the wicket as Cosier vainly attempted to reach the crease. That was in the very first over.

Bob Willis, Chris Old and Ian Botham then exploited the movement both in the air and off the seam and suddenly Australia were 53 for seven. The tailenders managed to double the score and the total rose to 116. Bob Taylor picked up five catches behind the stumps. The two spinners bowled one over between them.

We hardly made a better start. I came in first wicket down with Gooch caught in the gulley. Rodney Hogg was the bowler causing problems. I regarded Hogg as bowling at the same speed as Lillee had done in the Centenary Test. Boycott and I progressed slowly, only 38 runs coming in about an hour and a half, then Hogg came back for a second spell and Boycott edged a lifter to Kim Hughes at third slip. The relief on the Australian faces at the removal of the everlasting Yorkshireman was plain to see. Brearley sent in Bob Taylor as nightwatchman. I appealed against the light, failed to get anywhere; tried a second time, failed again, but third time lucky and we finished the first day 60 for two.

On the second morning the atmosphere was very humid. Bob Taylor and I, Bob just sticking a straight bat to everything, took the score above a hundred. I had 75 out of the total of 111 when I was very unlucky to be caught off a thick edge. Trevor Laughlin shoved an arm out and the ball stuck to his hand. He must have been as surprised as I was! Mike Brearley went cheaply, but Gower and Botham added the best part of a hundred for the sixth wicket and we had a very good substantial lead.

Australia, with hundreds by Yallop and Hughes, got themselves back in the game. We needed 170 in the fourth innings. Boycott and Gooch managed to reach 16 without loss by the close of the fourth day. Hogg soon removed Gooch on the last morning, no runs having been added to the overnight total. Then total disaster: I ran out Boycott, though Peter Toohey's fast throw from the covers which hit the stumps was also to blame. Mike

With an Australian companion in a lighter moment.

Brearley joined me and soon left. At lunch we were 82 for three, David Gower having come in.

After lunch we quickly got on top of the bowling. 88 runs came in a little over an hour and half and the game was won. I received the Man of the Match Award for my scores of 75 and 74 not out.

What naturally pleased me was that, having been left out of the England team for six consecutive games and then getting the last place in the side to Australia, I had re-established my England position at the first opportunity.

I shall pass by the Second and Third Tests with just brief details. The second game at Perth was won by 166 runs. It was a low scoring game, Gower's 102 being the only three figure innings. Rodney Hogg took ten wickets. I was out to a foolish hook in the first innings. In the second innings I was well in control, totally confusing Yallop by unorthodox shots, then I attempted to sweep the spinner, Bruce Yardley, from outside the off stump and gave a simple catch to bat-pad.

We lost the Third Test—Mike Brearley decided to open with Boycott and drop Gooch down the order, but both Brearley and Boycott failed. So did everyone else. Hogg picked up another ten wickets, this time for just 76 runs. The ball kept low throughout the game and the inevitable experts said that England's batsmen failed because we played back, instead of forward.

So to the Fourth Test and the reason for this chapter. It was at Sydney in the second week of January. The heat was intense, something over 100 degrees. Australia's win had put some life into the series, though the Packer media circus was going full blast in opposition. Australia had the misfortune to have their wicketkeeper, MacLean, hit in the eye whilst batting in the nets before the game and whether or not he would play was the main news story.

Mike Brearley won the toss and decided to bat. We made a terrible start and never recovered. Rodney Hogg, who suffers from asthma, had to leave the field after just an over or two due to breathing difficulties, but his new ball partner, Alan Hurst, had Geoff Boycott out for 8. I arrived and lasted two balls. Hurst bounced his second delivery to me, I couldn't resist a hook and, though I timed it well, was caught at deep square leg. I won't go down the rest of the scorecard: we were all out for 152.

When Australia batted, Willis quickly succumbed to the heat. Botham and Hendrick, our other two seam bowlers, also found the temperature very trying and Australia gained a lead with just two wickets gone. Despite the conditions we managed to keep the home batsmen from building a huge score; in fact of the later players only young Allan Border really made an impression. He was left stranded with 60 not out when the final wicket fell.

The Australian lead on first innings was 142. The sun had baked the ground causing cracks and the ball pitched taking lumps out as it did. It was clearly going to help the spinners more and more.

We began our innings before lunch. The first ball, from Hogg, was not anything special, I was sitting watching with my pads on, but wondering about lunch and trying to keep cool. There was a sudden shout. Boycott was trapped leg before to the first ball of the match.

I walked to the middle. I can't remember what Mike Brearley said, but it was probably just:

"Twasack, don't hook."

I tried to control my instincts and play a straight bat to everything until I had the pace of the wicket. I must admit I was very lucky not to be given out leg before to Geoff Dymock just before we went off for lunch. In the afternoon Brearley and I risked nothing. The captain was keeping his beady eye on me, so experimental shots were dispensed with. The runs were taken off the loose deliveries—with the heat building up the bowlers tired quickly and the quicker ones bowled in spells of three overs, we were still in the days of eight ball overs.

The partnership topped a hundred and we were near to avoiding an innings defeat when, Yallop, in desperation, brought

Ian Botham who was a major force in the 1978/79 series.

on Border to bowl left arm spin. Border got one to turn and shoot through. The surprised Brearley was bowled. Gooch, who had done so little in the previous Tests, had to survive for about half an hour until stumps and this he did. We were 133 for two, my score being 65.

The heat had affected both Gower and Botham and although they would, if necessary, crawl to the wicket, everything depended upon me when play began on the fourth day. The weather was even more unpleasant than on the previous days, the humidity being that much more intense. The flies seemed to be everywhere. The umpires carried flysprays which were in frequent use—too frequent for Yallop's liking. He complained that I was causing delays by going to the umpire for another dose of spray. The sweat ran off me as I slowly built up my innings. I chatted to myself as if I was alone on a desert island, rather than surrounded by concrete stands filled with spectators (well, half filled with spectators; the Packer publicity had its effect on the crowds).

Gooch survived about an hour and a half, so his 22 took over two hours in all. He was caught by Graeme Wood at silly mid-off. By lunch I was 87, and David Gower had quickly hit 18.

The afternoon heat proved too much for one of the TV cameramen. Up on some scaffolding, he suddenly fainted and with a dull thud dropped to the concrete below. This incident upset my concentration and I had only just regained it when Hogg arrived with the new ball. My total was then 95. I took two fours off his first over and therefore reached my century. I hit several lofted drives and was fortunate that they landed in empty spaces.

I gave myself a severe talking to and settled back into defence with the occasional attacking shot at the bad ball. Gower couldn't restrain himself and after a fluent 34, nicked Hogg to the wicketkeeper. Four wickets were now down and Botham, the last recognised batsman, came in. The total showed we were only 95 runs ahead. Botham couldn't fathom Higgs, who was getting ever more help from the pitch. He muddled his way to 6 and was caught.

Celebrating after my innings at Sydney.

Leg before wicket, bowled Hogg.

By now I was plain knackered—I don't know if that comes with or without a 'k', but however it is, I was! I played a half hearted shot to Hogg, the ball rapped my pad and my innings was over. I had batted almost ten hours for 150 runs. Graham Yallop claimed it was an innings he will never forget. Neither will I.

The following day the remaining four England wickets went down for 42 runs. Australia were then set 205 to make in 265 minutes. Even before we had started the game Mike Brearley had inspected the wicket and pronounced that the side batting last would struggle to make 200. His prediction as to the way the pitch would wear had proved correct and I doubted if their target was possible. Yallop clearly decided that the only course of action for him was to hit out. Rick Darling and Graeme Wood put on 38 for the first wicket, but Gooch then took a dive in the gulley and caught Darling. Wood embarrassingly ran himself out—he shouted and ran, his partner paid no attention and both batsmen found themselves at the bowler's end. The middle order collapsed and John Emburey, who had the spinner's place instead of

Edmonds mopped up the tail. We won by 93 runs. I'm not going to pretend I can list previous Test Matches in which a team that was nearly 150 behind on the first innings came back to win, but it's the only time that it has happened in the Tests that I've played.

We had now secured a three to one lead in the series and whatever happened in the two remaining matches England would hold on to The Ashes. If this match had been lost the series would have been wide open.

The Australian press gave their team a hard time and when we won the Fifth Test, at Adelaide, by 205 runs, the fight went out of them. We won the Sixth Test by nine wickets.

Liz and Simon flew out to Australia for the final part of the tour, which kept me cheerful—four months is a long time to be away from home and family.

AUSTRALIA v ENGLAND

Played at Sydney, January, 6, 7, 8, 10, 11, 1979
England won by 93 runs.

ENGLAND

1	G. Boycott	c Border b Hurst	8	lbw b Hogg	0
2	*J.M. Brearley	b Hogg	17	b Border	53
3	D.W. Randall	c Wood b Hurst	0	lbw b Hogg	150
4	G.A. Gooch	c Toohey b Higgs	18	c Wood b Higgs	22
5	D.I. Gower	c MacLean b Hurst	7	c MacLean b Hogg	34
6	I.T. Botham	c Yallop b Hogg	59	c Wood b Higgs	6
7	G. Miller	c MacLean b Hurst	4	lbw b Hogg	17
8	+R.W. Taylor	c Border b Higgs	10	not out	21
9	J.E. Emburey	c Wood b Higgs	0	c Darling b Higgs	14
10	R.G.D. Willis	not out	7	c Toohey b Higgs	0
11	M. Hendrick	b Hurst	10	c Toohey b Higgs	7
	Extras	b 1, lb 1, w 2, nb 8	12	b 5, lb 3, nb 14	22
Total			152		346

1-18 2-18 3-35 4-51 5-66 6-70 7-94 8-98 9-141

1-0 2-111 3-169 4-237 5-267 6-292 7-307 8-334 9-346

Bowling	O	M	R	W	O	M	R	W
Hogg	11	3	36	2	28	10	67	4
Dymock	13	1	34	0	17	4	35	0
Hurst	10.6	2	28	5	19	3	43	0
Higgs	18	4	42	3	59.6	15	148	5
Border					23	11	31	1

AUSTRALIA

1	G.M. Wood	b Willis	0	run out	27
2	W.M. Darling	c Botham b Miller	91	c Gooch b Hendrick	13
3	K.J. Hughes	c Emburey b Willis	48	c Emburey b Miller	15
4	*G.N. Yallop	c Botham b Hendrick	44	c and b Hendrick	1
5	P.M. Toohey	c Gooch b Botham	1	b Miller	5
6	A.R. Border	not out	60	not out	45
7	+J.A. MacLean	lbw b Emburey	12	c Botham b Miller	0
8	R.M. Hogg	run out	6	(9) c Botham b Emburey	0
9	G. Dymock	b Botham	5	(8) b Emburey	0
10	J.D. Higgs	c Botham b Hendrick	11	lbw b Emburey	3
11	A.G. Hurst	run out	0	b Emburey	0
	Extras	b 2, lb 3, nb 11	16	lb 1, nb 1	2
Total			294		111

1-1 2-126 3-178 4-179 5-210 6-235 7-245 8-276 9-290

1-38 2-44 3-45 4-59 5-74 6-76 7-85 8-85 9-105

Bowling	O	M	R	W	O	M	R	W
Willis	9	2	33	2	2	0	8	0
Botham	28	3	87	2				
Hendrick	24	4	50	2	10	3	17	2
Miller	13	2	37	1	20	7	38	3
Emburey	29	10	57	1	17.2	7	46	4
Gooch	5	1	14	0				

Umpires: R.C. Bailhache and R.A. French

Toss: England

Close of Play: 1st day: Australia 56-1 (Darling 35*, Hughes 15*); 2nd day: Australia 248-7 (Border 31*, Dymock 0*); 3rd day: England(2) 133-2 (Randall 65*, Gooch 6*); 4th day: England(2) 304-6 (Taylor 3*, Miller 16*).

CHAPTER 9

Changes at Trent Bridge

The constant whirl of Test Matches, One Day Internationals and overseas tours became even more hectic and confusing in the winter of 1979/80 when the Australian Board of Control made its peace with the Packerites and England were sent to Australia for the second consecutive winter. The programme hurriedly cobbled together—the first time a touring side had had to cope with a Test series combined with a triangular One Day series under floodlights and some ordinary first-class matches mixed—was really too much to expect.

From my own viewpoint, the failure of England's recognised opening batsmen meant that I was hastily being converted into an England opener. I hit 97 in the opening match of the tour, partnering Geoff Boycott and combating the rejuvenated Jeff Thomson on a green wicket at Brisbane. From then on, it was downhill and I lost my place in the England side for the final Test and in the One Day Internationals. The latter decision was a very harsh one. I scored 49 in the first game, opening with Mike Brearley, and we beat West Indies, whose attack comprised Roberts, Holding, Garner and Croft. In the second game I made 28, opening with Boycott and we beat Australia including Lillee and Thomson by three wickets. I then hit 42, opening with

Boycott in the third game; again we beat Australia. In the fourth match, I was out first ball, a nasty delivery by Andy Roberts and I was then, after one failure, dumped down to no.5. England's opening pairs for the remaining matches had partnerships of 41, 31, 5, 13, and 40. This compared with 79, 71, 78 and 0 for the four opening stands in which I was involved. The figures speak for themselves.

Cricket has its ups and downs. The upshot of all this was that I was not selected for any of the Tests at home in 1980. My thoughts therefore returned to Trent Bridge and Nottinghamshire. I had a very successful summer with the bat in county cricket, but in a way I have a Rip Van Winkle side—I woke up to find the Trent Bridge I knew in 1975 and earlier completely changed in 1980.

In my blinkered world of dressing room, on the cricket ground, in the nets and home, the two major changes were the creation of a 'Cricket Manager' and a new style of leadership. In my whole career as a professional cricketer, the incident I found most unpalatable, (is that the right word? or should it be incomprehensible?) occurred in my fourth or fifth season. I'd hit one of my patches when nothing went right. There aren't any cricketers I know who haven't suffered the same, it's just that my heights and troughs seem to be somewhat larger than most of my colleagues. At any rate I was sent for by the County Committee, given a talking to, told to buck my ideas up or else my contract would not be renewed, all of which was, I suppose, fair comment. At the end I was told that in their opinion I wasn't trying. That final comment was a bitter blow. Ever since I could remember I wanted to do nothing with my life but play cricket. I wanted to be a batsman and score runs. I wanted to be the best fieldsman in England. I can be quite honest and say I went away and cried. I suppose the reader might find that ridiculous. Other, more outgoing players might have started a heated argument, or in extreme cases, marched out and never come back. I just had the stuffing knocked out of me. I couldn't understand anyone making

Ken Taylor, who was appointed Notts manager in 1978. I was to cause him many sleepless nights.

such a remark.

In time it all blew over. I might brood over things for a bit, but I'm not one to hold grudges. The point of my story is that Notts had appointed a Cricket Manager to run the team and his job was to form a buffer between the players and the committee, which he did. Of course we were very lucky to have Ken Taylor as the manager. If football is anything to go by, managers are usually square pegs in round holes. Ken was definitely a square peg in a square hole. The difference between Ken and most other managers in sport was that he hadn't switched overnight from being player to being in management. He had spent the best part of twenty years as a manager in industry.

I dare say I caused him as many, or more, headaches than the majority of other players on the staff. My brain doesn't always function in the same logical sequence as other cricketers.

The second change was the dropping of Mike Smedley as captain and the appointment of Clive Rice. I've jumped a step. Jack Bond came in 1974 as captain-manager and stayed one season. It didn't work out. He was unable to command a place in the Notts side on his playing ability alone and he did not see eye to eye with some of the cricket committee on other matters. In 1975, Mike Smedley was appointed captain. A very competent county batsman, conscientious but on the quiet side, he tended to have a cautious approach to the game. It might have been because of his Yorkshire upbringing, but I think more likely the fact that he played for ten or more years with Notts at a time when we had won nothing and often been the chopping block for the other counties.

It had been intended that Clive Rice took over from Smedley in 1978, but Clive had signed for Packer and the appointment had been shelved. In the middle of 1979, Ken Taylor had switched captains, giving Rice the job. It was a sad time for Mike Smedley and he decided that he had no choice but to retire. Clive Rice led from the front. He was an attacking batsman and a very good seam bowler. He built up a great team spirit and the players

I'm not too certain what happened. Mike Harris looks on.

responded. My criticism of him, if I dare be so bold, was that he would decide on a set strategy for a day's cricket and charge ahead with it even when it seemed that disaster would be the only outcome. You just couldn't get him to change course suddenly.

One of the first things that Ken Taylor did, having settled in as manager, was to look at our strengths and weaknesses and decide how best to improve the latter. With Bob White coming to the end of his career, we were very short of the slower bowlers—the unexpected arrival of Richard Hadlee had given us the best opening attack on the county circuit. Ken Taylor found two players who had more or less been abandoned by their native counties; he backed his judgement and signed Eddie Hemmings and Mike Bore. The signing of Hemmings was a particularly astute move on the manager's part. I'd played against Eddie for Notts Seconds. He had been one of the outstanding schoolboy players of the 1960s and joined the Edgbaston staff, I assume, straight from school. Edgbaston of course was chock-a-block with overseas players. The mysterious registration of overseas players at that time was beyond my comprehension, but Warwickshire did seem to have rather more than their fair share. Eddie spent more time in the Second Eleven than he did in the Warwickshire First Eleven. As soon as Eddie arrived at Trent Bridge he made an impact with his bowling and when in 1982 the England captain was discussing the merits of the various off break bowlers, I said that they could not find anyone better suited than Eddie. He played in the Tests of 1982 and then went to Australia with me the following winter. Mike Bore is a left arm bowler who can bowl both medium pace and the slower stuff. Although he didn't have the same impact as Eddie, he was a very useful man to have in the side. In his final season or two he ran the Second Eleven.

Whilst on the subject of managers, I feel I ought to mention briefly the problems of cricketers having individual managers. After the Centenary Test of 1977, I was inundated with letters inviting me to speak at dinners and other functions, open shops, endorse a whole variety of products and so on. There seemed to be no one to advise me, in that, as far as I know, none of the players at Trent Bridge had employed 'a manager'. Hayters, the press agency, apparently did also act as managers for some players and offered to look after my business affairs. They of course were based in London. Mike Hall, my old captain at Retford, also offered his services and I accepted his offer, preferring to deal with someone I'd known for years, rather than an agency in London.

The authorities at Trent Bridge didn't quite know the best way of handling a player who had a manager; I hadn't a clue. Without going into the ins and outs of the matter, it didn't work. With the knowledge I have now I would have approached the business from a different angle. I'm not a mercenary guy. Anyone can say that, but I'm sure the fact that I refused to sign for Packer and later refused to go to South Africa, makes that point clear. On the other hand it is foolish to miss out on sponsorship deals and the like—to state the very obvious a cricketer's career is only half one's working life.

"Where have you been?"

"I took Megan to school, you know I did."

Liz put on her 'I don't quite believe you' look.

"It was my foot."

An inadequate answer that got me nowhere.

"I went to the ground to see Sheila. She says it's an inflammation of a ligament in the sole of my foot—the pain I get when I bend my foot running."

"Peter phoned to ask what had happened to you."

"You sure? I bumped into him in the pavilion; he didn't say anything."

"Not that Peter; Peter Wright of Gunn & Moore."

"It must be Thursday. I was supposed to go and select my bats for the season. I'll go after lunch."

Peter Wright had succeeded Reg Simpson as Managing

Director of Gunn & Moore's, a few years back. He was one of the leading lights in Nottingham local club cricket and in the 70s had played quite often for Notts Seconds. A naturally cheerful person, I normally tested his cheer to the limit on my annual visit to the bat factory.

In my early days I used a relatively light bat, but with experience I found that a bat weighing around 2lbs 10ozs was better. With this slightly heavier bat I can just lean on the ball and it pierces the field; the lighter bat doesn't drive the ball at the same speed and this gives time for the fielders to cut the shot off. When I remember Gary Sobers' technique, he used the bat more like a golf club and ended his shot with the bat round his neck. Modern players don't do that, they lean into the shot, give the ball a punch and score that way. Chris Broad, Clive Rice and, to an extent, Tim Robinson have great back lifts. This helps them play straight and they adopt the method of punching the ball—it's more common with taller cricketers.

The first thing I look at in choosing a bat is the straightness of the grain. There should be between six and ten grains across the blade.

About five years ago I felt that I would do better with a shorter bat, because I am below average height. I experimented with a shorter handle, but this didn't work, since I have my hands wide apart for some shots. I therefore decided to take a little off the blade. I now find that reducing the blade by about a quarter of an inch suits my style of batting. One or two players use a long handle in county cricket; this provides a greater leverage, but I don't know of any county batsmen who use a shorter blade.

I've inserted that little piece on bats to explain why Peter Wright and John Knight—that's the man with the carpentry tools—don't like me turning up at Gunn & Moore's without an appointment. It can take the best part of a morning to fit Randall to a bat, or a bat to Randall.

"I'd better give Peter a ring, apologize and see if they've got time for me this afternoon. I've nothing else on, have I, Liz?"

I was more concerned about my foot than my bat—you can't take that to the carpenter's. We had to report back for training in a fortnight. Then there was the book to finish.

"What are we going to do about the book, Liz?"

"I told you to get on with it. How much time are you going to have once the season starts? I'll tell you. None."

"I've been through most of Mum's scrapbooks and made a lot of notes and I've got the stuff I put into Simon's tape recorder, or whatever it's called. D'you think that's enough?"

Liz's brow furrowed. She was thinking. Someone's got to do the thinking in our family.

"Go to Gunn & Moore. Sort your bat out. It shouldn't take more than an hour and a half. You'll be passing Trent Bridge on the way home. Stop off at the ground, take all your book gubbins and see what Peter in the library's got to say."

"Who's picking Megan up from school?"

"Never mind about that, Mrs. whatsit up the road'll do it if the worst comes to the worst."

I put the file and the tape recorder in the car. Liz came out after me.

"I'll phone the library Peter and tell him to expect you about half past three, so if Peter Wright suggests going round the corner for a drink, don't!"

It was nearer four when I drove through the Hound Road gate at the cricket ground and through the little green door into the library.

I won't bore you with the detailed conversation. The upshot of the discussion I had with Peter was that Liz would type my notes into acceptable English, ditto the tapes. I would make notes on half a dozen more matches, then in spare moments in hotels or at home in the evening I could read through the typed draft and correct, or rejig as necessary. I was in a much happier frame of mind when I drove back home for tea.

Surplus to England's requirements, in the winter of 1980/81 I went with Kevin Saxelby to Western Australia. Liz and the children also came. I was player-coach to North Perth. The job involved playing cricket at weekends and coaching a couple of evenings in the week. The standard of cricket was much higher than club cricket in England. The matches were arranged for two days each, with one side batting on the first Saturday and the other a week later. There were single innings of 80 or 90 overs each. The weather in the area around Perth was very reliable and you could pretty well guarantee the wicket from one week to the next, unlike Melbourne, for example, where rain can unexpectedly descend. The youth team of the club played on the same pitch as that used for the main Grade matches.

I stayed with Wally Edwards, captain of the North Perth Club. He had played in one or two Tests during John Snow's tour to Australia. Wally is a complete cricket nut and despite the fact that North Perth is an amateur side, they had developed a great

Celebrating my birthday with Wally Edwards.

team spirit. The social life was unbelievable. I had a great time and fitted in very well with the club cricket scene. When we weren't involved in cricket Sax and I had to do labouring jobs to earn our keep and for weeks on end we seemed to be digging trenches.

A couple of games stick in my mind. There was a brilliant innings by Graeme Wood in temperatures well above 100 degrees; in contrast we did have a rainy day for the North Perth v Melville game; Dennis Lillee was the opposition captain. I square cut his first delivery for four. He invited me to square cut the next ball which I promptly miscued into the wicketkeeper's gloves. The rain continued all day, but we ignored it and played on, the only reason being that there was a women's match on the adjoining pitch and we weren't going to be defeated by the weather whilst the ladies struggled on. Afterwards of course it transpired that the women continued for exactly the same reason!

I returned to England for summer 1981 on top of the world. The amount of cricket in Perth had just been enough to keep me in practice without turning me stale. On the other side of the Pacific, the England team had been beaten fair and square by the West Indies. The sad news had been the death of Ken Barrington whilst on duty as England's manager. He had been a great help and guide to me on previous tours.

My ambition was to return to the England side—several of the England batsmen who had gone out to the Caribbean had returned with tarnished reputations and as I saw it there was another opportunity for me.

The Australians were England's visitors in 1981. The three One Day Internationals were scheduled for the beginning of June, prior to the First Test, which would be held at Trent Bridge. I did relatively well in the early county games, both Championship and One-Day. When the 13 man squad was picked for the One Days I was in the team, but the selectors gave the last batting place in all three matches to Jim Love—the four other batting specialists were Boycott, Gooch, Gower and Gatting. England lost the rubber two matches to one. When it came to the first two Tests, Woolmer was given Love's place.

On a personal level the first half of the 1981 summer was one of disappointment, but as the season moved into July, Notts looked likely candidates to take the Championship title. Interest therefore shifted from International to county level.

Our run of success really began at Trent Bridge when Worcestershire were the visitors in mid-July. It was before the days of Radford, Hick and Rhodes. Worcestershire were not the force they later became. The wicket was very hard, almost lethal. Glenn Turner alone in the first innings, and Younis in the second survived for long. With Clive Rice hitting 152 and myself 65 we gained a large first innings lead and went on to win by ten wickets. The following game, with Yorkshire, had a very similar pattern. This time Clive made 172 and myself 87. Yorkshire collapsed to Hadlee in the first innings, but a revival led by the unknown Hartley in their second innings left us needing 115 off the final twenty overs. Paul Todd and John Birch opened the batting and put on 84. I went in and ran myself out, but we won by eight wickets.

Lancashire came to Trent Bridge—for some reason we had three successive home games—and were also beaten by eight wickets. Interest centred on young Fowler, who opened the Lancashire innings, but fell victim to Richard Hadlee in both innings. He was destined to make his England debut the following year. However he is not what I would describe as a natural opening batsman. He can't resist trying to hit the first ball out of the ground, rather in the fashion of Gordon Greenidge. Unfortunately he hasn't the ability of the West Indian.

Notts came unstuck at Hinckley. Leicestershire's opening pair added 206 on the first day and we never recovered. I made 101 in the second innings thanks to Roger Tolchard. I was backing up and Balderstone the bowler stopped in his run up and removed the bails. On appeal the umpire gave me out, but Tolly over-ruled the decision and I continued my innings.

The West Indian Sylvester Clarke had me leg before for a

With young Simon and three cubs on the playing field at Cropwell Bishop.

duck when Surrey visited Trent Bridge, but Hadlee and Rice overwhelmed Surrey and we won by an innings.

An interesting wicket had been prepared at New Road for our return game with Worcestershire. There was less than quarter of an hour's play on the Saturday. At lunch on Monday we were 97 for six; Rice ordered the tail to hit out and then declared with the total 170 for nine at ten to four. It was the Championship or bust for our skipper. He opened our bowling with Hadlee and Hemmings. Eddie took a wicket with his first delivery. Worcestershire were all out by the close, Eddie bowling without a break from the score box end. On the final morning Worcestershire relied almost entirely on spin. I hit a quick fifty before running myself out—yes again! Rice declared and set a target of 239. Richard Hadlee quickly dismissed the first three batsman at a cost of 17 runs; Hemmings and Bore took care of the rest and we were 27 points ahead at the top of the table with five matches to play. Rice's flair had won us that game, but it nearly lost us the following one. This was against the second in the table, Sussex. A win for either side effectively was worth double points.

Sussex made 208, then our batting simply fell to pieces. We were 60 for seven. The redoubtable Basher Hassan of the unmistakable stance hung on and with a few blows from Eddie Hemmings we just reached three figures. Hemmings and Bore opened the bowling in the second innings which will give an idea as to the pitch.

In the end we wanted 251 to win. Todd and Robinson played out a single over from Waller on Monday evening, then play started promptly on the last morning. By tea we were 144 for three; Basher was 72 not out and Rice 37 not out. Imran got me first ball, caught behind. After tea Rice and Hassan took the score to 174, then in quick succession both batsmen were out. Hadlee took a six off Barclay, but in that bowler's next over was caught attempting another. A cautious man would have told French to bat out time, but no, Rice wanted the runs. Three more wickets went down and we still needed 41, Hemmings and Bore being the last men. They had five overs to face against the formidable Garth Le Roux at one end and Imran at the other. I didn't reckon we had a hope. The light, which had already caused one break in play, was dreadful, but somehow the two prevented Sussex getting those winning points—although we didn't know it then those points would have given Sussex the title.

The Warwickshire match which followed was my best game of the summer. It was played at Edgbaston, which is the four star hotel of the county circuit. Few matches have been so remarkable during my career. On a pretty miserable Saturday, Amiss was feeling frisky and hit 83 before being caught by Basher at bat-pad five minutes before lunch. I should explain that by this time in my career I had moved from the covers into the slips. Rice was first slip, myself second, John Birch at gulley and Basher at bat-pad. Though I say it myself we had, with of course Bruce behind the wicket, a very good close catching combination.

Humpage hit out and Warwickshire made a very creditable 331 off 99 overs. We began our innings on the second day and Rice's orders were, attack. Unfortunately both openers went cheaply, Robinson being run out—I don't remember that being my fault. I came in and hit both Willis and Hogg for fours almost straightaway. By the time my old friend Doshi, who was immaculate as ever, got me out, stumped by Humpage, I had made 117 and the total was 210 for four. More important the runs were coming very fast. The 300 came up after 74 overs and with Hadlee hitting three sixes and three fours in quarter of an hour, Rice declared. We stopped for tea.

After the break Hadlee bowled from the score box end, Rice took the pavilion end. Dennis Amiss took strike, we were preparing for Warwickshire to score 150 that evening, put on some more during the last morning and set us a sporting declaration probably after lunch. Amiss took a single off Hadlee's first ball; Smith scored a single; Hadlee bowled a wide, but off the final ball of the over I managed to hang on to a mistimed drive, which Amiss edged into the slips. Rice in his second over had

The Notts championship squad of 1981.

Smith caught bat-pad by Basher and without a run being added I took a second catch to remove Andy Lloyd. The score was seven for three. There was no revival. The score rose to 30 for seven. Bob Willis, the Warwickshire captain, made 11, but the all out total was 49. It was inexplicable. Our final innings began at ten past six and by ten to seven we had hit 79 of which Paul Todd made 52—poor Hogg in his single over sent down three no balls which were hit by Toddy for 4, 4 and 3.

I don't intend to go ball by ball through the remaining three matches of the season. All were played at Trent Bridge and all provided us with decisive wins. Sussex also were very successful and when the last points had been counted we won by just two. The title was claimed on Monday September 14, the second day of the Glamorgan game, just after lunch. Todd hit Malcolm Nash for four to level the scores, then rather an anti-climax, Nash bowled a no-ball to finish the game. It was the first time in 52 years that the county had won the Championship. I remember Reg Simpson, Chairman of the Cricket Committee and the captain of the team in the 1950s, standing with tears in his eyes, next to Clive Rice and waving from the players' balcony to the crowd gathered below. I can't remember who said what, but we certainly celebrated that night!

WARWICKSHIRE v NOTTINGHAMSHIRE

Played on the County Ground, Edgbaston, August, 22 and 24, 1981
Nottinghamshire (24 pts) beat Warwickshire (8 pts) by eight wickets.

WARWICKSHIRE					
1	D.L. Amiss	c Hassan b Rice	83	c Randall b Hadlee	1
2	K.D. Smith	lbw b Hadlee	4	c Hassan b Rice	3
3	T.A. Lloyd	c French b Hadlee	32	c Randall b Hadlee	1
4	+G.W. Humpage	c Randall b Rice	65	c Robinson b Cooper	6
5	Asif Din	b Cooper	0	c French b Hadlee	1
6	P.R. Oliver	c French b Cooper	34	c French b Cooper	14
7	A.M. Ferreira	c Rice b Hadlee	40	c Randall b Hemmings	1
8	G.C. Small	lbw b Rice	1	c Cooper b Hemmings	3
9	*R.G.D. Willis	not out	33	c Rice b Bore	11
10	W. Hogg	b Hadlee	2	c Bore	4
11	D.R. Doshi	not out	12	not out	1
	Extras	b 9, lb 12, nb 4	25	lb 2, w 1	3
Total		(9 wkts dec)	331		49

1-23 2-130 3-134 4-141 5-235 6-236 7-242 8-283 9-297

1-3 2-7 3-7 4-15 5-19 6-22 7-30 8-42 9-48

Bowling	O	M	R	W	O	M	R	W
Hadlee	28	9	59	4	9	6	8	3
Rice	29	5	104	3	6	2	8	1
Cooper	20	3	70	2	7	3	17	2
Bore	8	3	20	0	3.2	1	8	2
Hemmings	14	2	53	0	8	4	5	2

NOTTINGHAMSHIRE					
1	P.A. Todd	c Smith b Hogg	13	not out	52
2	R.T. Robinson	run out	32	run out	12
3	D.W. Randall	st Humpage b Doshi	117	(4) not out	1
4	B. Hassan	b Ferreira	24		
5	*C.E.B. Rice	c Small b Doshi	50		
6	J.D. Birch	st Humpage b Doshi	20		
7	R.J. Hadlee	b Ferreira	32	(3) c Humpage b Small	11
8	+B.N. French	lbw b Ferreira	1		
9	E.E. Hemmings	c Lloyd b Doshi	2		
10	K.E. Cooper	not out	0		
11	M.K. Bore				
	Extras	lb 3, nb 9	12	lb 1, nb 2	3
Total		(9 wkts dec)	303	(2 wkts)	79

1-16 2-122 3-170 4-210 5-250 6-299 7-299 8-301 9-303

1-62 2-75

Bowling	O	M	R	W	O	M	R	W
Willis	7	1	26	0	4.1	0	32	0
Hogg	9	1	34	1	1	0	17	0
Small	4	1	16	0	2	0	10	1
Ferreira	28	4	121	3				
Doshi	26.3	6	94	4	1	0	17	0

Umpires: H.D. Bird and J. van Geloven

Toss: Warwickshire

Close of Play: 1st day: Warwickshire 331-9d (Willis 33*, Doshi 12*).

CHAPTER 10

One in the Face

England had saved the Ashes whilst we were winning the Championship. I looked at the names of the cricketers picked to spend the winter touring India under Keith Fletcher—Mike Brearley had decided to retire from Test Cricket—mine was not among them. I would have enjoyed another trip to India, but I missed out and went instead for a second time to my friend Wally Edwards in Perth.

I don't know if fate has anything to do with the course of events. I was certainly very happy in Perth; things did not appear quite so jolly in India. There were doubts in the weeks prior to the visit due to the connection between some players selected by England and South Africa. These doubts were smoothed over, but it was not long before I received an invitation to go to South Africa with a rebel team. I refused, but several of the England squad in India accepted. I don't know the ins and outs of it, and I don't wish to, but it is clear that such a clandestine carrying on must have had some effect on the England team.

The rebels in South Africa were banned from Test cricket and this afforded me an opportunity to re-establish myself in the England team. I was given a chance in May 1982 in the modern equivalent of a Test Trial: M.C.C. v Indians at Lord's. I scored an

Simon during our stay with Wally Edwards.

unbeaten 130, but there was a pointer to the future in that Gower was given the captaincy.

When it came to announcing the squad for the two One Day Internationals Fletcher, the captain in India, was discarded and Bob Willis appointed England's leader. As I have mentioned previously it was a foolish decision to give this responsibility to England's strike bowler. England won both One Days with ease and when it came to the First Test, I determined to succeed. I came in with England struggling. The first three batsmen, Geoff Cook, Chris Tavare and Allan Lamb made 17 runs between them. The best partnership of the innings was 125 between myself and Phil Edmonds for the 7th wicket.

Edmonds, the Middlesex slow left arm spinner, is not everybody's cup of tea. He was the same age as myself, but the similarity ceases there. He had captained Cambridge University and played his first Test in 1975. He loved what I would describe as, if I knew what it meant, an intellectual argument. If someone made a suggestion he would take the opposite stance and more often than not win the debate, regardless of whether he genuinely believed in the cause for which he argued. If you do this too often it can get up people's noses. We roomed together on tour once or twice and people seemed surprised that we didn't fall out. The secret was that he wouldn't get far into a debate with me and I'd be totally baffled and unable to understand what he was on about. Unlike my slightly more brainy colleagues I didn't get into any frustrating arguments with him. On the whole I believe his wife suits him down to the ground.

Back to the Test, which was at Lord's. We won, but Kapil Dev enlivened the final day. He hit 89 in 55 balls and then took all three wickets to fall as England were left just 67 to make in the fourth innings. He's a fine cricketer.

It was just as well we did win that game, because the Second Test was ruined by rain—my Indian friend Dilip Doshi had me for nought with a beautiful ball which turned and bounced. I ought to have known all his tricks after our hours in the Trent Bridge nets.

The third and final Test, at The Oval, was drawn. I had a glorious partnership with Botham. He hit 208 in some tremendous time and one of his sixes, off Doshi, went through the pavilion roof. We added 151 together. The match drifted to a draw on a plumb wicket.

The second half of 1982 was centred on a series against Pakistan. Looking at the score of the first game, I see that I opened the England innings. I think some comedian in the press at the time, or perhaps later, imagined the Test Selectors at work. My name happened to be in the side chosen. They put ten of the eleven in their best batting position and then put me in the place which was left. If they were looking at twelve players, they put eleven of them in their best batting position and then made me 12th man. There's probably no truth in this at all, but if anyone went to the trouble of charting the batting positions of the principal England men between 1976 to 1986, I believe I would be the one going up and down and in and out more than any of my colleagues. Perhaps someone who reads this will spend the winter trying to disprove it!

It's nearer the truth to say that because I elected to remain committed to England rather than going off to Mr. Packer or to South Africa and because I have rarely suffered a major injury, I have weaved in and out of players with bans or bandages.

To confound everyone I actually scored a century in the Edgbaston Test against Pakistan. My opener partner was Chris Tavare, a man I would simply describe as a gentleman, though not beyond the occasional practical joke, as I was to discover when on tour with him.

Of course I failed as an opener in the Second Test and in the Third suddenly found myself at no.7. I ran myself out in the first innings and was given out leg before to a yorker from Imran in the second.

Many people told me that I was a certainty to go with England to Australia in the 1982/83 winter, but I err on the side of caution and did not search out my hat with the corks hanging off it until

Saturday September 11th, when the official announcement of the side was made: in fact we were down at Hove playing Sussex, so the corked hat had to wait a day or two. Eddie Hemmings was chosen to go to Australia for the first time and therefore also for the first time on my England travels, I had a county colleague in the party.

We flew to Australia in mid October. Willis was our captain, Gower his lieutenant and Doug Insole the manager. I didn't play in the opening game at Brisbane, but I was lucky that the First Test was arranged at Perth and that the crucial game prior to that match was also at Perth. The local Western Australian side contained a few notable cricketers including the wicketkeeper, Rod Marsh and Dennis Lillee. My two winters with Wally Edwards made me feel at home at the WACA, but I needed a good innings to ensure a place in the England side. I was batting down at no.6: Fowler and Tavare opened the batting, with Gower, Lamb and Botham all ahead of me in the order.

Allan Lamb was on his first tour with England. He had qualified for England by residence at the beginning of 1982 and had played in all six of the summer's Tests, but had failed completely against Pakistan scoring less than fifty runs in the three Tests. He had still been pencilled in as an automatic choice for the tour. He's a magnificent batsman. Just like Botham he's always battling and never concedes defeat, but he needs really tough opposition to bring out the best of him.

Being an old hand, Doug Insole decided I was the person to guide Lamb's first footsteps in Australia. Aeroplane trips are novel for the first hour or so and then get progressively more boring. The journey to Australia takes about 30 hours. Lamb's solution to the flight was to drink the bar dry—what would happen if he and Rodney Marsh were on the same plane I shudder to think. The pilot would be forced to keep stopping to fill up. Anyway we did eventually land somewhere in Australia. I had visions of carrying Allan off the plane, but as soon as he saw land approaching he started getting very excited. Everyone else is

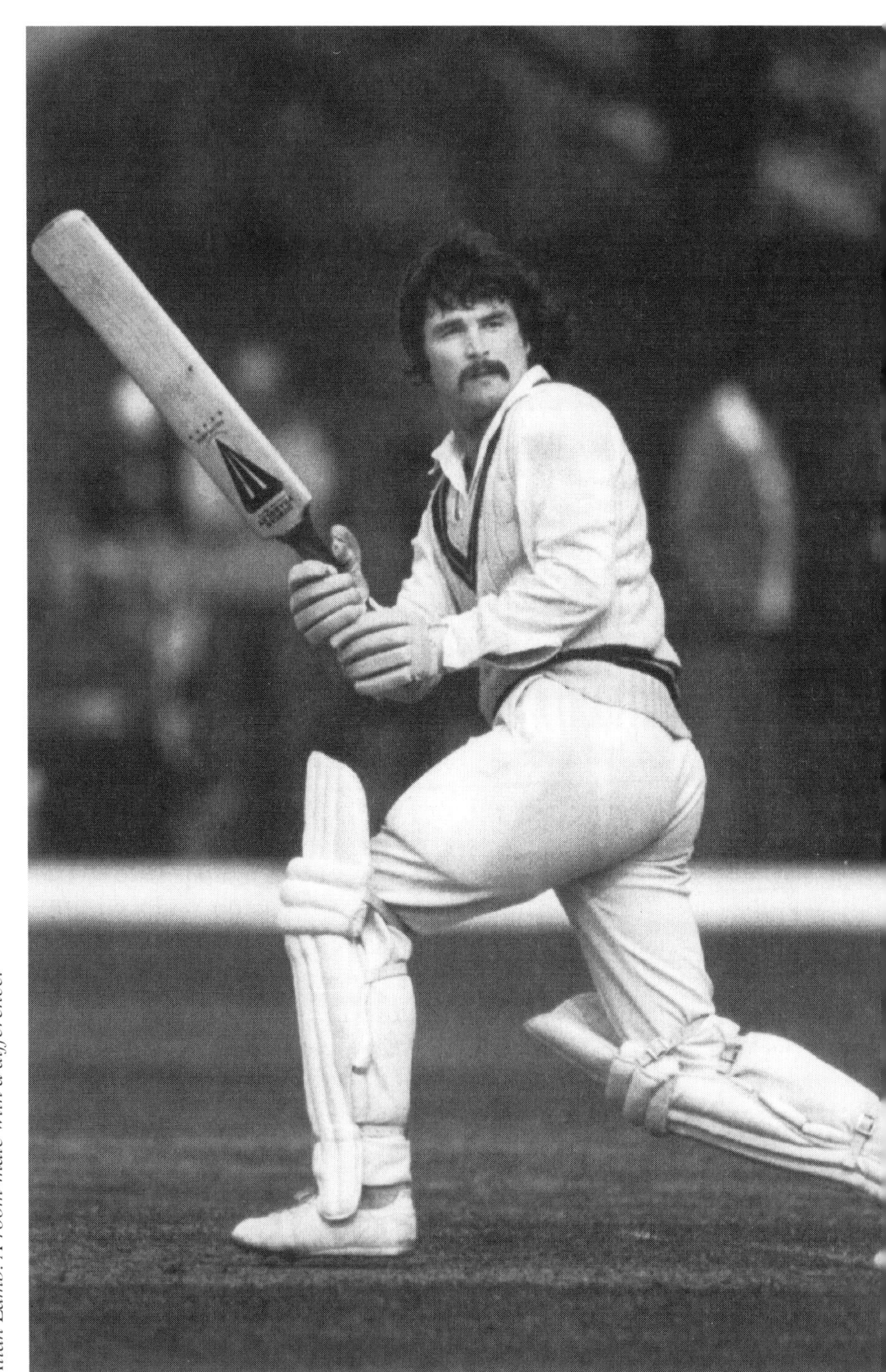

Allan Lamb. A room-mate with a difference.

shattered and longs to crawl into bed. Lamb's into the hotel and heads straight for the bar to have a few more drinks in celebration of his arrival.

I leave him to it and go up to our room. I'm sound off when there's a hammering on the door. Opening it, I watch Lamb lurch by and throw himself on the bed. His aim's somewhat confused and he lands on the floor. This has a temporary sobering effect and he picks up the bedside menu, grabs the phone and proceeds to order everything that catches his eye. Five minutes later he's dead to the world. Fifteen minutes later another knock on the door produces three trolleys laden with food. The waiters disappear. I feel obliged to eat as much as I can. It must have cost him a hundred dollars. Next day he's as right as rain and I'm wandering about with a bloated stomach. So you can see that Allan Lamb takes a lot of looking after; he's in to everything. His missus does a very creditable job. As a cricketer, there's few better.

Back to the cricket. What happened in the Western Australian match was that there were cracks in the wicket from the start. The first three innings amounted to 167, 156 and 197 with the only fifty coming from the long handle of Botham. So we began our final knock needing 209. Lillee got Tavare caught by Marsh for a duck; poor Chris was out in the first innings in exactly the same way for the same score. His partner Fowler manages a couple before Lillee disposes of him and in no time at all we're 82 for five; Gower and Lamb also having come and gone. Geoff Miller had been injured in the first innings but would probably bat, the others remaining were Bob Taylor, Derek Pringle, Norman Cowans and Bob Willis. In other words things were looking rather hopeless. However Pringle was not overawed and we added 105 for the sixth wicket. Alderman then bowled a magnificent spell. I was caught behind. Pringle, Cowans and the injured Miller also went, Alderman taking four wickets for seven runs in less than four overs. Bob Taylor between playing and missing scraped together the last five for victory: by one wicket.

This at least put us in a cheerful mood for the First Test,

A moment to think. Batting with David Gower in the Test Match at Sydney. We added 122.

which began four days later. England's main selection problem was who should open the innings. In the end Willis left out Fowler and chose Geoff Cook to partner Tavare. When it came to deciding which of the final twelve should be twelfth man, Willis opted for a seam attack with one spinner; this meant that Eddie Hemmings was omitted from the side. Poor Eddie felt right down in the dumps. I know because I've been there before!

Greg Chappell, who had been reinstated as Australia's captain, won the toss and put us in. Lillee soon had Cook confused, but David Gower joined Tavare and they were still together at lunch. There are few more elegant batsmen than Gower and he had made 72 out of 95 when he attempted a shot through mid wicket, but misjudged it sending a catch to Dyson at short square leg. Lamb and Botham put bat to ball, Lamb hitting a tremendous straight six which crashed against the sightscreen and Botham connecting with two or three hard hit fours, but they came and went. Chris Tavare remained unbeaten—perhaps I ought to say simply 'remained'. Whilst I batted at the other end, I don't believe he made a single run. Stuck on 66, he was, for well over an hour.

So we finished for the day at 242 for four, I was 32 and Tavare still 66. The great excitement of the second morning was, would Tavare score a run and when? The wicket was fast and suited me. I played most of my strokes off the back foot and reached fifty gliding a ball from Lillee between third man and long leg. Tavare did eventually score a single and just missed the world record in Test cricket for the longest period without adding to his score. In the end Bruce Yardley removed both of us. Chris Tavare switched to attack and mistimed a sweep. I was caught bat-pad by Wood. Yardley, the off spinner, has an unusual action. He spins the ball with the second finger as opposed to the normal off spinner who uses the forefinger. By and large I find no difficulty in playing off spin, but Yardley could make the ball come through much quicker than one expected.

Our tail added some useful extra runs, but when the score

reached 400 for eight sometime after tea, a gang of drunken yobs began running on the outfield. One of them starting jeering at Terry Alderman, then another actually hit the fast bowler, who grabbed the youth and threw him to the ground. Some other fielders rushed to assist Alderman, but in the struggle, he dislocated his shoulder. It proved so serious that he couldn't play again during the series. Greg Chappell led his players off the field and various fights broke out between rival sets of supporters. It took the police about quarter of an hour to restore order. The game resumed. Our innings soon ended and Australia batted out the final hour of play without loss.

We had a bit of a debate as to whether Australia ought to be allowed a replacement for Alderman, rather than simply a sub fielder. With Australia back at full strength (having the Packer players available) we were regarded as the underdogs, but I feel it would have been a very nice gesture to allow a replacement. It would have set a good tone for the series, whatever its outcome. The press painted the likes of Chappell, Marsh and Lillee as the hard men of cricket, but as I had found out five years before—was it really five years since the Centenary Test?—they were capable of gestures worthy of the game. Our management decided not to make the offer; Australia did not ask and that was the end of the matter. A pity.

Australia made a useful start, but with the openers and Border gone, the spotlight turned to Greg Chappell. He simply took poor Norman Cowans apart. Norman's name will always be connected with shoes. We both took the same size in footwear and had been issued with a regulation pair for 'state occasions'. I can't remember where it was, but Norman and I shared a room. We were leaving one hotel for another. I packed my bags and went down to the coach. The manager checked the bodies. One missing. It was Norman. Eventually someone went and dug him out. He'd lost his shoes. You can guess the rest of the saga. I'd packed my shoes; forgotten and then put what I thought were my shoes on, only they were Norman's. There's some old music hall

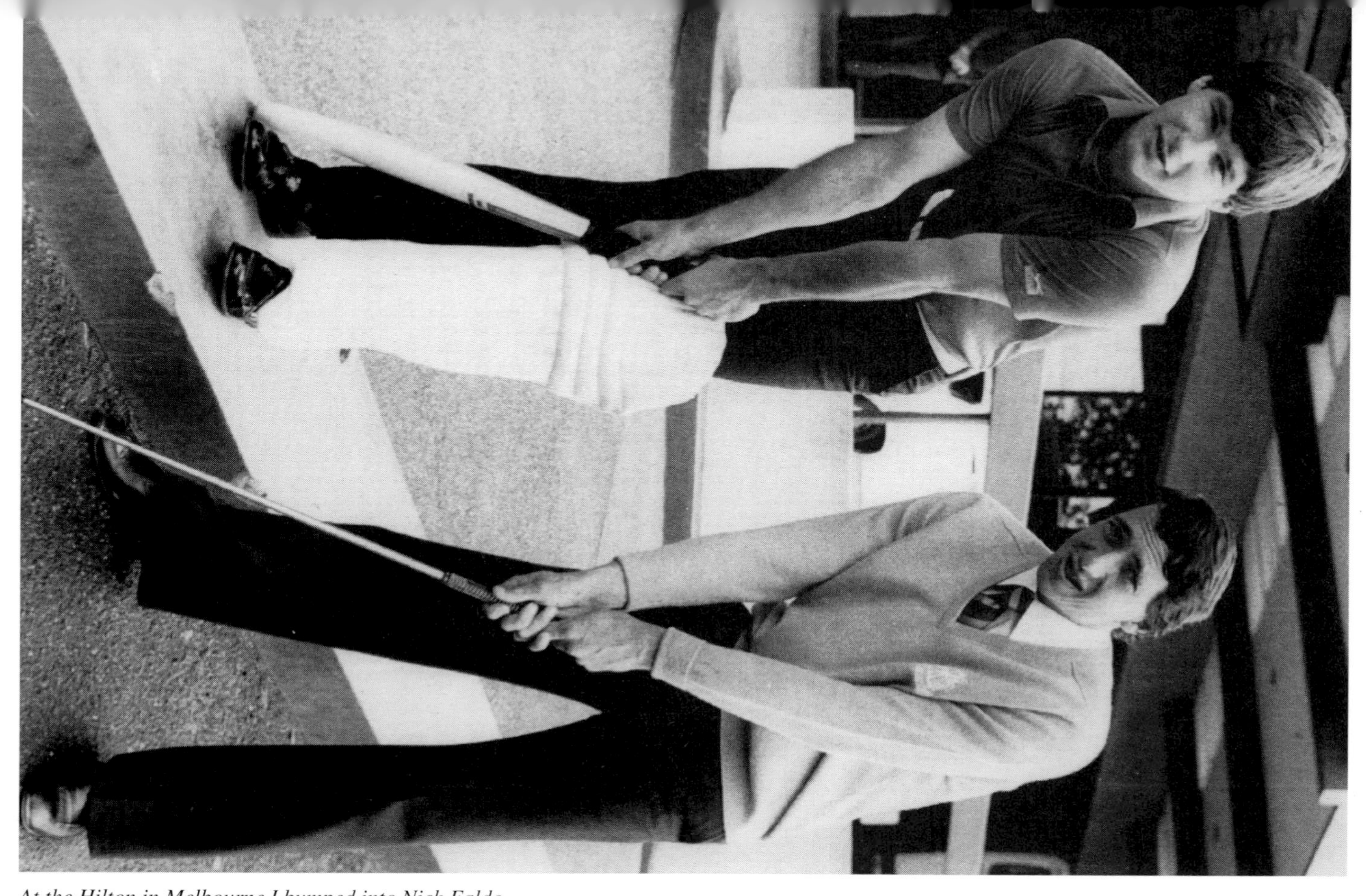

At the Hilton in Melbourne I bumped into Nick Faldo.

song that Grandad used to sing, something about brown boots, while all the rest wore black and morning suits. It was a case of trainers, while all the rest ... It wasn't until we were unpacking at our next hotel that the mystery of Norman's shoes was finally solved. I think he's forgiven me.

Back at the Test, Chappell's innings was enjoyed almost as much by the fielders as by the spectators, he made 117 which included several splendid sixes. Australia finished that Sunday on 333 for six. We then had a day off.

Tuesday was Geoff Lawson's day. He played correctly and made a well deserved fifty. Australia's total went above ours, but they batted a man short and their overall lead when Bob Willis had Yardley caught was only 13. It was lunchtime on the fourth day. Without Alderman, Chappell invited Lawson to open the bowling in partnership with Lillee. Lawson got one to lift, Cook mishit and the ball went into the slips, where Border took a very nice catch. Neither Gower nor Tavare batted very confidently, but whilst Gower scored runs, Tavare got stuck again. Lillee had Gower leg before. After tea, Tavare fell to the high bounce of Yardley—Tavare had batted over two hours for nine. Botham came in and quite simply missed the second ball he faced. We were 80 for four and the experts were predicting defeat. I came in to join Allan Lamb. As in the first innings I found the wicket to my liking and with Lamb batting well the scoreboard was soon moving nicely. Fatally Lamb attempted to glide a leg side delivery from Lawson wide of Marsh, but the wicketkeeper moved too quickly and Lamb returned to the dressing room. Willis sent out Bob Taylor and together we batted out time.

Bob Taylor reached 31, then was bowled off his pads by Yardley. Geoff Miller came in, couldn't resist a wide delivery from Yardley and was out without scoring. Derek Pringle, who had scarcely made a run on the tour, arrived. Chappell immediately took the new ball, but we both survived until the lunch interval. After lunch I had not got going, the heat was affecting me I think, and at 115 I played a ball on to my wicket.

The game by now was virtually safe. Norman Cowans and Pringle added fifty plus for the last wicket, which removed any vague hopes Australia still entertained and the match drifted to a draw. I won the Man of The Match Award. Greg Chappell blamed Australia's failure to win on poor catching, but their bowling without Alderman was thin and, although we didn't realise it at the time, Dennis Lillee was not fully fit in the second innings.

So we survived the First Test. Because of the injuries to Alderman and Lillee, Australia brought in Rackemann and Thomson for the Second Test, but it was Lawson who dominated the game with six wickets in the first innings and five in the second. The problem of going in at no.6, as I was now doing was amply illustrated in this game, because I effectively ran out of partners and with hitting out the only solution, was caught on the long leg boundary, hooking. We were all out for 217. Australia built a commanding lead and we lost by seven wickets. The Third Test, at Adelaide, was very much a repeat of the second, though this time we batted after Australia and were then forced to follow on. The margin of Australia's victory was eight wickets.

With three Tests played, two lost and one drawn, we went off to Tasmania for what was described as a couple of holiday fixtures. The first was a three day game at Hobart. I suppose I should have been warned by the flight to the island. The plane fought its way through great flashes of lightning and a howling gale which kept us going up and down like a yo-yo. The match was interrupted by rain, but with declarations we were set 264 at somewhat more than one a minute. Poor Tavare spent three quarters of an hour making a single and this put tremendous pressure on myself and Gower. However we hit 99 for the fifth wicket and were still together when the game was won. I made 90 not out in a little over an hour and Gower, exactly 50.

We went up to Launceston, the other major centre of Tasmanian cricket, for a One-Day game. The Fourth Test was only a few days away and no one seemed very keen to play. As I'd

With Bob Taylor and Bernard Thomas after my injury at Launceston.

made a lot of runs in the three day game, I was clearly down to be rested, but volunteered to take part when everyone was trying to avoid the captain's eye.

We won the toss and Bob Willis decided to field. The wicket was a little dodgy. Robin Jackman and Vic Marks exploited it and Tasmania were all out for 112 from 42.5 overs of a 50 over match. All we needed was two runs an over. However the Tasmanian team contained none other than Michael Holding. Holding had not taken the three day game very seriously and bowled at half pace off a reduced run. Whether someone on the Tasmanian Cricket Board had given him a dressing down, or whether he simply felt frisky I don't know, but we watched his first over to Geoff Cook with awe. Cook survived. Tavare viewed the situation from the other end and the unknown bowler partnering Holding dismissed poor Chris for a duck. I came in—promoted to no.3. Was everyone else hiding in the showers, or was it my imagination?

Holding was even more fearsome in his second over, made the ball lift, hit Cook on the finger and gulley accepted an easy catch. It was in Holding's third over that I found myself at the wrong end. The second delivery, or was it the third, hit a length. I got my feet in position, my bat vertical and head over the ball. It simply shot up, brushed my gloves and went straight into my mouth.

The ball split my upper lip, damaged my nose and teeth; the blood spurted everywhere. I managed to stay upright and tried to take a few paces towards the pavilion. Bernard Thomas and Eddie Hemmings rushed out. I was escorted to the local hospital. They patched me up and I was well enough to go back to the team's hotel. I phoned Liz back in England, simply to reassure her that it wasn't quite as bad as it would appear on the press photographs.

As the reader can imagine, a blow on the face from Holding at something near 100 m.p.h. is likely to sap a batsman's confidence. The first thing I had to do was to learn to bat with a visor—I had been wearing a helmet for a couple of years, but did not like the idea of the visor, which I felt restricted one's vision. Bernard Thomas suggested that I go to a local squash club and try playing squash wearing the helmet, plus visor. By doing this I became accustomed to the visor. Whilst England battled through the Fourth Test at Melbourne—and won by three runs—I was busily trying to adapt to my new style helmet. It had only been four years previously when Mike Brearley had gone in to bat with his strange dog ear type helmet and everyone had laughed at him. Nowadays a county batsman without a helmet is looked on as unusual, Viv Richards being one of the few who have ignored the new fashion.

The Fifth and final Test, which Australia only required to draw to take the Ashes followed almost directly after the fourth game, but at Sydney. I had been pronounced fit and took the place of Graeme Fowler. Fowler, who had failed in the first innings of the fourth match, had batted well in the second innings and was into his 50s when Hogg hit him on the foot and cracked a bone in his big toe. He was not fit for selection.

The pitch looked worse than it was, so Greg Chappell, on winning the toss, decided to bat. The Australian innings lasted until teatime on the second afternoon. They scored 314 and were in no hurry. Geoff Cook and Chris Tavare opened, against Lawson and Hogg—Thomson was reserved for first change. Tavare was clean bowled, middle and off, in the third over for a duck. David Gower came in. Cook was unsettled; Hogg's pace beat him and he was caught by Chappell. Allan Lamb was the new batsman. The following over he shouldered arms to Lawson and was bowled. We were 24 for three.

It was not a situation which I would choose for my return to cricket after my facial disagreement with Holding, but I had no choice. There was an hour to go before stumps and Lawson, Hogg and Thomson were as chirpy as they were ever going to be. By the close we had added 52 runs. The visor gave me confidence, I found my eye as keen as ever and there was nothing more than usual astray with the feet.

On the third morning Yardley came on and immediately started to make the ball turn and lift. Off spinners have never caused me much of a headache and by using my footwork I soon had him unable to decide where to pitch the ball. David Gower was also treating the bowling with disdain. My score overtook Gower's and I was first to the fifty. Thomson returned to the attack. Fatally I became overconfident. I played at a wide half volley on the offside and dragged the ball onto my stumps. We'd added 122 and I'd made 70. After that the wickets fell much too regularly; Botham failed; Gower was also out for 70. Eddie Hemmings hit 29, before being caught bat-pad and the total was 237. Whatever happened we had no hope of winning the game. The old experts, O'Reilly and Laker, criticised the England spin attack, namely Miller and Hemmings, in Australia's second innings, Australia making 382, but when England went in for the final knock with only a draw to play for, Eddie rebuilt his reputation. Geoff Cook was out for 2, Eddie came in as nightwatchman. He made 95, the last twenty or so in partnership with me. It was sad that Eddie just failed to reach his hundred. I reached 44, but it was Geoff Miller and Bob Taylor who batted out the final overs and saved the game, if not the Ashes.

The tour ended with a long session of One Day Internationals, first the Benson & Hedges World Cup and then a series of three games in New Zealand.

AUSTRALIA v ENGLAND

Played at Perth, November 12, 13, 14, 16, 17, 1982
Match Drawn.

ENGLAND					
1	G. Cook	c Dyson b Lillee	1	c Border b Lawson	7
2	C.J. Tavare	c Hughes b Yardley	89	c Chappell b Yardley	9
3	D.I. Gower	c Dyson b Alderman	72	lbw b Lillee	28
4	A.J. Lamb	c Marsh b Yardley	46	c Marsh b Lawson	56
5	I.T. Botham	c Marsh b Lawson	12	b Lawson	0
6	D.W. Randall	c Wood b Yardley	78	b Lawson	115
7	G. Miller	c Marsh b Lillee	30	(8) c Marsh b Yardley	0
8	D.R. Pringle	b Lillee	0	(9) not out	47
9	+R.W. Taylor	not out	29	(7) b Yardley	31
10	*R.G.D. Willis	c Lillee b Yardley	26	b Lawson	0
11	N.G. Cowans	b Yardley	4	lbw b Chappell	36
	Extras	b 7, lb 9, w 2, nb 6	24	b 5, lb 11, w 2, nb 11	29
Total			411		358

1-14 2-109 3-189 4-204 5-304 6-323 7-342 8-357 9-406

1-10 2-51 3-77 4-80 5-151 6-229 7-242 8-292 9-292

Bowling	O	M	R	W	O	M	R	W
Lillee	38	13	96	3	33	12	89	1
Alderman	43	15	84	1				
Lawson	29	6	89	1	32	5	108	5
Chappell	3	0	11	0	2.3	1	8	1
Yardley	42.4	15	107	5	41	10	101	3
Border					7	2	21	0
Hookes					1	0	2	0

AUSTRALIA					
1	G.M. Wood	c and b Willis	29	c Taylor b Willis	0
2	J. Dyson	lbw b Miller	52	c Cowans b Willis	12
3	A.R. Border	c Taylor b Botham	8	not out	32
4	*G.S. Chappell	c Lamb b Willis	117	not out	22
5	K.J. Hughes	c Willis b Miller	62		
6	D.W. Hookes	lbw b Miller	56		
7	+R.W. Marsh	c Cook b Botham	0		
8	G.F. Lawson	b Miller	50		
9	B. Yardley	c Lamb b Willis	17		
10	D.K. Lillee	not out	2		
11	T.M. Alderman	absent, injured	—		
	Extras	b 4, lb 1, w 1, nb 25	31	lb 1, nb 6	7
Total			424	(2 wkts)	73

1-63 2-76 3-123 4-264 5-311 6-311 7-374 8-414 9-424

1-2 2-22

Bowling	O	M	R	W	O	M	R	W
Willis	31.5	4	95	3	6	1	23	2
Botham	40	10	121	2	6	1	17	0
Cowans	13	2	54	0	3	1	15	0
Pringle	10	1	37	0	2	0	3	0
Miller	33	11	70	4	4	3	8	0
Cook	4	2	16	0				
Lamb					1	1	0	0

Umpires: A.R. Crafter and M.W. Johnson

Toss: Australia

Close of Play: 1st day: England 242-4 (Tavare 66*, Randall 32*); 2nd day: Australia 30-0, (Wood 12*, Dyson 12*); 3rd day: Australia 333-6 (Hookes 35*, Lawson 4*); 4th day: England 163-5 (Randall 45*, Taylor 3*).

CHAPTER 11

I master Hadlee: for once

I shall have to begin this chapter with an extract from Richard's book "Rhythm and Swing". Richard comments:

"But at the top of the pile (of my special favourite batsmen) is my old Nottinghamshire team-mate Derek Randall, who managed to satisfy my wicket-taking desires no fewer than nine times. Because I played with him for so many years on the county circuit—and bowled to him an awful lot in the nets—I had the advantage of knowing the way he played. He was a fidgety player and a chirpy character who gave the impression of being very confident when, in fact, he was quite insecure and hopelessly nervous in the dressing room before going out to bat. For the first few overs, he rarely looked comfortable but, if he could overcome that phase, chances were he'd play a fine innings ..."

I cannot deny that Richard has bowled me out more often than any other bowler—in fact eleven times in first class matches plus several more in One Days—but you can prove anything with statistics. The other side of the coin is that Richard was in a class of his own so far as New Zealand bowlers were concerned and the Tests I played against New Zealand were at the very peak of Richard's career. Enough said.

If there was ever a more determined and dedicated cricketer

In the space of seven deliveries, Richard dismissed Tavare, Gower and myself.

than Richard Hadlee, I haven't met him. We all saw his list of 'targets' which he had in his coffin. I suppose most of the Notts cricketers had some similar lists though only in the mind, but Richard had, not only the talent, but the type of character to set himself goals and allow nothing to divert him from the path.

New Zealand were scheduled to come to England in 1983, but only after the World Cup. Having played in 1979, I was keen to represent England in this third competition. I was picked for the 14 man England squad, but when it came to the final eleven, Mike Gatting took my place. The selectors were clearly doubtful about my ability to succeed in the One Day game. At any rate, I didn't get the chance and England failed to reach the Final, which was between India and the West Indies. To everyone's surprise, India who had come to England as outsiders, won the trophy with ease.

I didn't get downhearted; I trained hard and must have impressed Peter May with my enthusiasm, because I found myself picked for the First Test against New Zealand. This time Mike Gatting found himself out in the cold.

The game was played at The Oval in the middle of July. Willis won the toss. The sun had produced a hard, dry wicket which seemed ideal for batting, so that's what he did. Unfortunately Hadlee seemed to have other ideas. We were all out for 209. Graeme Fowler was trapped by Hadlee, leg before, having scored one. As I said before, he is not designed by nature to be an opener. Gower, coming in first wicket down, received a very good delivery from Hadlee and was clean bowled. We were 18 for two. Lamb got himself out, then Tavare, who had opened with Fowler, was hit in the mouth by one which Hadlee got to lift. Bearing in mind my experience just a few months before I did not like the look of that. This was the point when I had to come in; Botham was batting at the other end. Botham edged a ball from Hadlee on to his stumps and England were 116 for four. Tavare was deemed well enough to return, but the complete story was that England's later batsmen all failed and I was stranded with an unbeaten 75.

Willis and Botham bowled England back into the match.

Bob Willis and Doug Insole – the captain and the manager.

Richard Hadlee alone batted well and made 84 out of the total of 196. Fowler and Tavare put on over 200 for the first wicket in England's second innings, demonstrating how weak New Zealand's attack was once Hadlee had been overcome. Both of them made hundreds as did Lamb. I came in with the total 322 for four and nothing to play for—we won by 189 runs.

The first phase of the Second Test followed the game at The Oval. England failed after batting first. I was caught in the slips off Cairns who made the ball move away—Botham suffered in a similar way. Unlike the First Test, New Zealand's batting produced runs and they gained a lead of over 150. Gower hit a century in our second innings; it was not enough though and New Zealand won their first ever Test in England.

My failure in that game meant that Gatting was preferred for the Third Test: Fowler was also discarded, Chris Smith coming in. England won and therefore took a two-one lead in the series. Because of the World Cup, the rubber comprised four matches instead of three or five.

Trent Bridge was the venue for the final Test. I was in the squad, but assumed I would again be 12th man. It was the year of my Benefit and the Benefit Committee had arranged a champagne breakfast at the Victoria Club in Nottingham on the morning of the first day. I got up early and went to the beanfeast. Having shaken everybody's hand and chatted about nothing in particular, I drove down London Road and across the bridge into the ground. Being home territory to me I pottered into the familiar dressing room and began to wonder what I was going to do to while away the time, in between rushing on the field with vital bits and bobs.

I was totally resigned and relaxed. Quite unexpectedly Bob Willis announces that it has been decided to play an extra batsman and ignore David Thomas, the young Surrey left arm bowler. We won the toss, batted and once again the early batting failed, except for Gower, who was hit on the head by Hadlee—Gower was still ignoring helmets. When I came to the wicket at quarter past three, the score was 169 for five. Botham was at the other end. Botham greeted my arrival with a tremendous six over long off, Bracewell being the unfortunate bowler. The New Zealand captain, Geoff Howarth, decides that my presence demands the return of Hadlee to the firing line. Hadlee feeds me with deliveries to mishook, which I immediately do, but the ball lands out of harm's way. I'm tempted a second time and the ball goes sweetly to the boundary.

We stop for tea. Botham is 19, I am 14 and the total 198 for five. After the break we are at our most relaxed, runs come; we each reach individual fifties in the same over. Hadlee takes the new ball, but even he is unable to control us. In one glorious over I hit Richard for three successive fours. 164 runs are added in 32 overs. The report noted:

"Botham's first century in 23 Test innings and Randall's virtuoso performance on his home ground were two of the happiest aspects of an enjoyable match. Botham hit with tremendous power and the stand between these two certainly dictated the course of the rest of the match."

In the end Hadlee did dismiss me, but I had made 83 runs and was caught in the covers. Botham was out one run later. It was my golden opportunity to score a Test century at Trent Bridge. As it turned out, a chance that was never to recur, but I shan't forget that afternoon's batting and when it ended England were 362 for seven.

Our innings finished some minutes before lunch on the second day. New Zealand's batting stretched from then until nearly lunch on the third day, but they only amassed 207 runs. Their scoring rate was little more than half ours and the bowler who received the cheers was neither Botham nor Willis, but Nick Cook. Cook had come into the England team by mistake. Just before the previous game (the Third Test at Lord's), Phil Edmonds ricked his back getting out of his car. Cook was playing for Leicestershire at Chelmsford and was pulled out of the middle of the county match in order to come to Trent Bridge. A very strange state of affairs. He promptly took five for 35.

In this, his second Test, he picked up five for 63. Cook is a

"Don't worry lads, I'll sort it out," was Botham's comment when the next shower of mud was heading our way.

big spinner of the ball, but he doesn't possess the variation of flight and guile which slow bowlers require at Test level. My picture of him is sitting on a large stone in Australia, looking like a Chinese Emperor. A very relaxed character, whenever I bump into him he has a smile on his face—that doesn't sound quite right, but you know what I mean.

Although we gained a lead of over 200, Willis did not enforce the follow on. With only four main bowlers, he felt that they required a rest before demolishing New Zealand a second time. It's difficult to know exactly how to behave when you start the second innings 213 runs ahead, especially as in my case you were down to bat no.7. In theory we had something to bat for and that was the winter plane to New Zealand and Pakistan. In practice, Lamb made a very sound hundred, everyone else decided it was holiday time. None of the other ten made higher than 33. New Zealand required 511 in eleven hours. It was never on the cards, but Hadlee had the last laugh hitting 92 not out and like myself, just missing a hundred at home. Now was the time to wait for the announcement of the England touring party. On the whole I think the honours were even between Richard and myself in that series—despite his presence I had scored 194 runs at an average of 38.80, and had played a major part in two of my three Tests.

A week after the final Test, the side to tour New Zealand and Pakistan was made public. It included all the eleven of that Test: Tavare, Chris Smith, Gower, Lamb, Gatting, Botham, Bob Taylor, Nick Cook, Willis, Cowans and myself, plus just four others, Graham Dilley, Neil Foster, Graeme Fowler and Vic Marks. The two main comments were that we had no reserve wicketkeeper and that Phil Edmonds had been omitted. The tour comprised virtually nothing except Tests and One Day Internationals—the additional fixtures were two or three games against New Zealand provincial sides.

We didn't leave England until the end of December, which gave me a Christmas at home—a rare event in recent years. The flight was across the United States with a stop over in Fiji. Here the temperature, humidity and mosquitoes made the visit exceedingly uncomfortable and I was pleased to reach the more pleasant surroundings of Auckland. I didn't play in the opening game, but in the warm up game before the First Test, I hit an unbeaten hundred and the selectors decided to continue the policy of playing seven batsmen. Graeme Fowler was the batsman omitted. It had been raining in buckets a few days before the game. The turf was so sodden that we were unable to use the outdoor nets and helicopters were brought in to try and dry the playing area. As there was a howling gale, this seemed somewhat unnecessary.

The first day of the match however was warm and sunny. Howarth won the toss and chose to bat. For the first day and a half the bowlers were in total control. We dismissed New Zealand for 219 and Bob Willis celebrated his 308th Test wicket, which passed Fred Trueman's record. Our first five batsmen all failed and the score was 115 for five. Lance Cairns, not Richard Hadlee, had taken all five wickets. I arrived to join Botham. He had given a couple of chances and was not looking too happy. We batted through to tea.

Suddenly it was Trent Bridge six months before. Between tea and the close Botham and I added 121 runs. We went gaily on our way when the match resumed in the morning and by the time Botham hit a vertical six, which Jeff Crowe had the daunting task of catching, we had added 232 in 201 minutes. The score was 347 for six. I batted on with the aid of the tailenders and England's total came to 463. Last out, I had reached 164. It's true Richard Hadlee captured my wicket, but at great cost and I think it's also true to say that I didn't offer a single chance during the six hours I batted.

Batting with Botham is marvellous. Anyone who has played in a team with him knows that his presence alone makes the team buzz. He inspires the rest of us to play above our ordinary game. This series in New Zealand was ruined by newspaper stories of sex and drugs. New Zealand is such a quiet sort of a place that a larger than life character such as Botham is bound to attract publicity. Any story which could be linked to him was sure to make the headlines. The journalists were therefore searching for the least whiff of scandal, which they could blow out of all proportion. Botham took it all in his stride and in the process received the flak, which in many cases ought to have hit other members of the team. He was a big man. The rest of us could hardly be described as innocents abroad, and I suppose we were lucky that we had someone of Botham's stature to protect us.

''Don't worry, lads, I'll sort it out,'' was his comment when the next shower of mud was heading our way.

We had gained a lead of over 200 on the first innings, but the wicket became progressively easier and our three and half man attack never looked likely to dismiss New Zealand for a modest score a second time: Botham had suffered a leg strain whilst batting and although he bowled a good few overs he had little venom in his delivery.

The Second Test was on Hadlee's home ground at Christchurch. I don't like making excuses but the pitch was designed for Hadlee. We were in trouble before we started. Both Dilley and Foster were injured and in desperation our manager co-opted 'Lester' Pigott, the Sussex seam bowler, who was coaching in Wellington.

New Zealand decided to bat first. Pigott picked up the first wicket, when I caught Edgar at leg slip. By lunch the total was 87 for four. Pigott bowled well and Cowans, who had found difficulty keeping a length in the earlier games, also looked effective. The position started to change in the middle of the afternoon when Hadlee arrived. In one over from Botham, Richard hit four fours. Pigott, bowling at the other end, was hit mercilessly. Why Willis kept the poor lad on, I couldn't understand. It destroyed Pigott's confidence and whilst it didn't lose us the match, it did nothing for the rest of the players. Suddenly, the damage done, Willis awoke to the position, brought himself and Cowans back and finished off the innings. New

Zealand had made 307 instead of 207.

As if to ram home our confusion, when we had quarter of an hour or so to bat on the first evening, Howarth quickly brought on their left arm spinner, Boock, and he took Fowler's wicket just before the close: we had decided to go into the game without a single spin bowler!

Overnight rain meant that play couldn't begin until half past four on the second day—Saturday. When it was judged fit to start, the atmosphere with heavy clouds overhead was just Hadlee's cup of tea. In the space of seven deliveries, Richard dismissed Tavare, Gower and myself. At stumps we were 53 for seven. At quarter past twelve on the third day, Monday, we were all out for 82, Mike Gatting carried out his bat, more by luck than judgement.

Fowler and Tavare took the England second innings score (we had been asked to follow on) to 8 without loss by lunch. Matters soon altered when play restarted; as I walked to the wicket the score board displayed 31 for five. Botham and Gatting had gone for nought, Boock taking both wickets. Bob Taylor joined me and we managed to double the score in a stand for the seventh wicket. In the end Hadlee got me again, but at least I made the highest score of either England innings. We were all out for 93.

The Third Test of the series was arranged directly after the Second, at Auckland. The pitch was absolutely dead. We had learnt a lesson from Christchurch and dropped a batsman in favour of a spin bowler, Vic Marks took the place of Mike Gatting.

New Zealand won the toss and batted and batted and batted—over eleven hours, Wright, Jeff Crowe and the wicketkeeper, Smith, all made hundreds. They declared at 496 for nine. Fowler was dismissed first ball by Hadlee, but Chris Smith, who had taken Tavare's place, showed that he could occupy the crease for as long as was needed. Chris's batting is in the Geoff Boycott mould and in this innings he showed it. He is talented, but not up to the standard of his brother.

He spent seven and a half hours over his 91. Things got so

In one over from Botham, Richard hit four fours.

dull that Hadlee actually switched style and bowled slow left arm to Smith. The most cheerful part of the match was the partnership I shared with Botham. He was suffering from a damaged foot and came in at no.7. Other than that the match dribbled away to a draw.

The visit to New Zealand ended with three One Day Internationals. We won two and the series, with New Zealand finding consolation from victory in the third game. The first was at Christchurch. We batted first on a dodgy pitch; Hadlee removed Lamb, Botham and Gatting in the space of seven balls. I however won this round against the formidable Richard, hitting 70 off 85 balls, before he had me caught. My innings was the only one of the match over fifty and I also received the Man of the Match Award. In the Second One Day, I can also claim victory over Richard. I was 25 not out when we beat New Zealand at Wellington by six wickets. In the third game I was bowled by Boock for 11.

Having finished our New Zealand programme we flew to Pakistan, or should limped be the word to describe the journey. The plane was 60 hours late and this was serious indeed because, without any preliminaries we began the visit with a Test Match.

We had about 48 hours on the ground before the Test at Karachi started. The difference between conditions in New Zealand and Pakistan was so vast, not only the actual grounds and wickets, but everyday living; we had an armed escort accompanying us on our travels, as well as in front of the dressing room door. The food, which can be a problem, was on this trip good and Bernard Thomas filled in with bottled water and banana sandwiches when required. Pakistan were without Imran or Javed, but the key to the series proved to be Abdul Qadir. A bowler of legbreaks and googlies he had come to England with the 1982 Pakistan touring side. In the early matches on that tour, Qadir had baffled county batsmen, but the Test wickets were not designed to help him and he was not so much of a threat to our England players.

It was a different story in Karachi, where the First Test of our present visit was staged. The pitch assisted Qadir, but not to excess, we were simply unable to read his googly, since his action seemed identical to that for the ordinary leg break. When someone asked me at what point in Qadir's delivery I realised which way the ball would spin, I admitted it was when I turned round and saw my wicket broken. I batted quarter of a hour and made 8 in England's first innings of 182. In the second innings I survived an hour and made 16. Both innings ended 'bowled Qadir'. Gower was the only England batsman to make any progress and that because he was left handed. We ought to have lost by ten wickets, but the Pakistani batsmen in their second innings had an attack of nerves and Nick Cook took five for 18. We lost by three wickets. My method of dealing with Qadir in England had been to use the sweep, but Zaheer, the Pakistan captain, was wise to me and had two or three fielders ready for that shot.

This was Pakistan's first win at home against England and there was naturally great jubilation, though because of the tense political climate the crowds coming to watch the cricket were nothing like they'd been in India on my previous trip.

Five days after our defeat we were at Faisalabad for the Second Test. The difference was that Bob Willis, Ian Botham and Norman Cowans were not available for selection through injury or illness. While players were dropping out, those of us who were fit had a brief tour of some of the historical sights of Pakistan. My single memory was of being diddled out of 15 rupees at some fort or other. The fort was surrounded by a moat which contained some ten feet of water. The fort's tower must have been the best part of 150 feet high and from our vantage point we could see a slim figure up on the battlements. The guide said that if each of us would give 15 rupees he would persuade the man on the tower to dive into the moat. We parted with our cash and waited for the feat to be performed. I watched him dive and a second or two later the splash as he hit the water and then the figure emerge from the moat. It was death defying stuff. Puzzling over this I wandered away from the official group. All was revealed! Our guide had placed us in such a position that, having seen the man leap off, he then disappeared from view behind a projecting piece of masonry. Wandering off, I found that he landed on a ledge and that a second diver jumped from a window fifty or sixty feet below.

March 12 found us in Iqbal Park, Faisalabad with twelve fit men—the selectors didn't have too many problems picking the side. We wanted to win to level the series, but the Pakistan authorities produced a pitch on which the bowlers hadn't a hope of taking a wicket.

Behind the scenes, the newspapers had now broken the so-called drug scandal story, but Botham had flown home and Faisalabad is a place so cut off from normal communications—a phone call to England would occupy the best part of a day to organise—that the rumours and counter-rumours had little effect on us. The main concern was ensuring that our little band contained enough players fit to see out the match. Zaheer decided to bat first. Graham Dilley was feeling far from his best; he opened the bowling with six no balls in the first over.

It is unnecessary to go into any further detail of the game. It was boring. Even David Gower, who was leading in place of Willis, spent over a day on his 152. I did manage the only six of our innings which totalled 546.

The Third Test was an unhappy game for me. I was out caught off Qadir in both innings; I know I tend to complain when given out, but on both these occasions the umpiring was somewhat suspect. The match itself turned out to be quite exciting: it was a pity very few people turned up to watch. Pakistan gained a first innings lead of just over a hundred, when their ninth wicket took the score from 181 to 342. Zaheer, who had injured himself when fielding, came in at no.7 and Sarfraz at no.10 hit 90. David Gower—is there any better batsman in England?—played brilliantly in our second innings and set Pakistan a reasonable target on the final day. They responded well and reached the stage where they required 99 off the final twenty overs with all wickets still intact. We looked on in amazement as they collapsed in a heap. Six wickets went down and it was left to Sarfraz to bat out time.

I shall have to close this chapter on a sad note. Within three months of returning from Pakistan, my career with England came to an end. In the first-class batting averages on the twin-tour of New Zealand and Pakistan, I stood second to David Gower and with an average more than double that of Allan Lamb and Chris Tavare, and almost double that of Mike Gatting and Graeme Fowler. Back in England that set of figures was cast aside. I was picked for the First Test against West Indies at Edgbaston, failed—as did Fowler, Gower and Lamb—and I was the one who was shown the door. It never opened again.

Trying to look at the situation from the selectors' angle, I still hadn't fully recovered in mind from being hit in the face by Holding. Although that had happened eighteen months before, one doesn't overcome such an accident in a matter of weeks. I realised that I still tended to back away from the very quick bowlers of Garner's calibre. On the other hand I was determined in my own mind to conquer this weakness. And I did. The double hundred I made against Derbyshire with Holding in their attack finally proved that, but by then, 1988, the England selectors had gone elsewhere. The principal reason however for the ending of my England career was, I feel, the change of England captaincy. Tony Greig, Mike Brearley and Bob Willis all encouraged me and seemed to want me as part of their ideal team. Three different captains, with three very different views on the leadership of England. When Gower took over, I realised I was not the sort of player he required. I'm not aware of the goings on at Committee level, but my feeling is that his opinion tipped the scales against me.

I'm sorry if this gives the impression of a moan, which I suppose it is in a way. For me of course it was the end of a fantastic period in my life: some people might say I was lucky to go on so many England trips and play in so many Tests.

A few players I've known have more or less given up cricket

when the opportunity of playing for England went, but I simply enjoy playing at whatever level and in 1984 was happy to continue at county standard.

At home with Liz and Simon just after the arrival of Megan.

NEW ZEALAND v ENGLAND

Played at Basin Reserve, Wellington, January, 20, 21, 22, 23, 24, 1984
Match Drawn.

NEW ZEALAND

1	J.G. Wright	c Cook b Botham	17	c Foster b Cook	35
2	B.A. Edgar	c Taylor b Botham	9	c Taylor b Willis	30
3	*G.P. Howarth	c Gower b Botham	15	run out	34
4	M.D. Crowe	b Willis	13	c Botham b Gatting	100
5	J.J. Crowe	c Taylor b Foster	52	lbw b Botham	3
6	J.V. Coney	c Gower b Cook	27	not out	174
7	R.J. Hadlee	c Gatting b Botham	24	c Lamb b Foster	18
8	M.C. Snedden	c Taylor b Willis	11	c Taylor b Foster	16
9	+I.D.S. Smith	lbw b Botham	24	b Cook	29
10	B.L. Cairns	c Gatting b Willis	3	c sub (Fowler) b Willis	64
11	E.J. Chatfield	not out	4	b Cook	0
	Extras	b 4, lb 9, nb 7	20	b 4, lb 14, w 2, nb 14	34
Total			219		537

1-34 2-39 3-56 4-71 5-114 6-160 7-174 8-200 9-208 — 1-62 2-79 3-153 4-165 5-279 6-302 7-334 8-402 9-520

Bowling	O	M	R	W	O	M	R	W
Willis	19	7	37	3	37	8	102	2
Botham	27.4	8	59	5	36	6	137	1
Foster	24	9	60	1	37	12	91	2
Cook	23	11	43	1	66.3	26	153	3
Gatting					8	4	14	1
Smith					3	1	6	0

ENGLAND

1	C.J. Tavare	b Cairns	9	not out	36
2	C.L. Smith	c Hadlee b Cairns	27	not out	30
3	D.I. Gower	c Hadlee b Cairns	33		
4	A.J. Lamb	c M.D. Crowe b Cairns	13		
5	M.W. Gatting	lbw b Cairns	19		
6	I.T. Botham	c J.J. Crowe b Cairns	138		
7	D.W. Randall	c M.D. Crowe b Hadlee	164		
8	+R.W. Taylor	run out	14		
9	N.G.B. Cook	c Smith b Cairns	7		
10	N.A. Foster	c Howarth b Hadlee	10		
11	*R.G.D. Willis	not out	5		
	Extras	lb 8, nb 16	24	nb 3	3
Total			463	(0 wkt)	69

1-41 2-51 3-84 4-92 5-115 6-347 7-372 8-386 9-426

Bowling	O	M	R	W	O	M	R	W
Hadlee	31.5	6	97	2				
Snedden	21	3	101	0	7	2	28	0
Cairns	45	10	143	7				
Chatfield	28	6	68	0	5	0	24	0
M.D. Crowe	3	0	20	0	6	1	11	0
Coney	4	1	10	0				
Edgar					3	1	3	0
J.J. Crowe					1	1	0	0

Umpires: F.R. Goodall and S.J. Woodward

Toss:

Close of Play: 1st day: New Zealand 212-9 (Smith 22*, Chatfield 0*); 2nd day: England 293-5 (Botham 103*, Randall 91*); 3rd day: New Zealand 93-2 (Howarth 11*, M.D. Crowe 8*); 4th day: New Zealand 335-7 (Coney 76*, Smith 1*).

CHAPTER 12

Two Benson & Hedges Finals

There can hardly be a greater contrast between two matches than our two visits to Lord's in the B&H Final, the first was against Somerset in 1982 and the second against Essex in 1989. In the first we were slaughtered and in the second won off the last ball.

We had begun the 1982 season full of confidence. Notts went to Lord's to play the M.C.C. at the beginning of May in what was really the Champion County versus The Rest of England. As a match it has never captured the public imagination, but it was regarded as an important occasion. For me the game has particular memories, not because I scored 84 runs, but because I returned the best bowling figures of my career. Rain caused so much interference that we were still batting in our first innings on the last morning. Rice declared with Notts still 138 in arrears; it was then up to Keith Fletcher, the M.C.C. captain, to knock up a hundred or so and declare leaving us a target. Richard Hadlee soon removed Geoff Cook the M.C.C. opening batsman, but Butcher and Gower settled in. The score reached 89 for one when the rain returned. We took an early lunch. Play restarted at half past one and Rice decided to put on the 'joke' bowlers to give them some quick runs. Tim Robinson bowled the first over after the resumption and gave away eight runs, I conceded eight off an over at the other end. Tim's second over went for four runs, then Butcher attempted a hook off my deadly bouncer and was caught by Birch. Richards the wicketkeeper came in and in my following over I had him snick a catch to Bruce behind the stumps. My final scalp was the great Gower. For some reason he was using Phil Edmonds' bat with the long handle and just managed to reach one of my wider deliveries, getting it right on the bat end. Bruce took another good catch and M.C.C. declared. I'd ended with figures of 3.5-1-15-3.

That's got precious little to do with the B&H Cup, but it does remind me of a photograph which was taken in the next game. We went straight from Lord's up to Old Trafford for the three day game against Lancashire. The best bowler in the Lancashire side was the West Indian Colin Croft. He bowls wide of the crease with a slingy action which sends the ball into the batsman and makes it difficult to pick up the line. I went to hook one which proved somewhat faster than I had anticipated. I missed the ball entirely and it crashed against my helmet. The following day I received a picture which clearly showed the imprint of the ball on the helmet and the camera man had captioned it: "Best wishes Colin Croft".

The intention of this chapter is however the Benson & Hedges Cup. The first match in the competition was at Northampton the day after the Lancashire Championship game—well it should have been, but we thrashed Lancashire in two days (despite Colin Croft) with an innings to spare, so we had a day at home. We were put in. Todd and Robinson struggled against Sarfraz and Griffiths. After three quarters of an hour we were 32 for two. Rice then joined me and we soon had the score moving quickly. Our partnership was worth 77 in about an hour. Birch and Hadlee continued the run spree and we made 234 for seven off 55 overs. Northants had a pretty good batting line up, including Cook, Larkins, Lamb and Steele. Mike Hendrick produced one of the best performances of his time with Notts—six for 33—and Allan Lamb alone was able to survive. At tea the Northants score was

47 for four off 24.1 overs with Lamb 11 not out. He hit out afterwards, making 95, but had no support.

We lost the toss in the second match and were again put in to bat. This was against Warwickshire at Trent Bridge. We made a terrible start. Gladstone Small got rid of me. He's not what you'd call a genuine fast bowler, but he can be sharp and moves the ball either way. This combined with his accuracy makes him a handful at any time. I can't understand why he hasn't played more frequently for England.

Basher Hassan and Richard Hadlee saved us from total collapse and some more accurate bowling by Mike Hendrick—he had figures of 9-3-19-3—produced our second B&H win.

Our third fixture was in Glasgow and was little more than a formality, though I must admit I didn't manage to score any runs. We met Lancashire in the fourth game. As both our counties had qualified for the knock-out section, it remained only to decide which would have the home fixture.

Yet again Clive lost the toss and we had to bat first, but this rather backfired on Lancashire because the light in the early evening became very gloomy and it is unpleasant batting against Hadlee and Hendrick even on a bright day. So, though we made a modest 216 for eight, Lancashire needed 53 off the last five overs with the best batsmen back in the pavilion. It was an impossible mission.

A couple of days after this game, Bill Thornley died. He'd been taken ill just before the match at Glasgow, but no one realised that it was anything serious. A quiet conscientious man he had acted as scorer for ten years. His place was taken by Les Tomlinson, who had been the second team scorer for several years. We quickly named him 'Foggy' after the character in the TV comedy, "Last of the Summer Wine". He was what I would describe as a self-educated man, full of home spun philosophy. His life had been spent as a nurse in a local mental hospital and he understood the workings of the mind. In his day he had been a very good wicketkeeper-batsman and just missed out on joining the playing staff at Trent Bridge. When Ken Taylor asked him to take over the First Team scoring, he felt it meant too much responsibility and therefore suggested that he do the job jointly with his friend, Len Beaumont, the former League footballer and cricket coach. So for the next few seasons we had joint-First Team scorers. Few jobs can be so unusual as that of county scorer. Not something I can do.

We were drawn against Leicestershire, at Trent Bridge, in the Quarter Finals. Richard Hadlee couldn't play due to a strain—I ought to have pointed out that due to back trouble Clive Rice could scarcely bowl all summer. This time Rice won the toss and decided to bat. Illingworth had gone back to Yorkshire and Roger Tolchard was the visiting captain. Our main worry was Andy Roberts. In fact we were so concerned about his bowling that, as is often the case, it was the bowlers at the other end who took the wickets. Our total of 156 all out owed a great deal to Basher Hassan; he opened the innings and hit 48. No one else reached 30.

Nottinghamshire in 1982.

It seemed a modest score, but Hendrick bowled brilliantly. His first six overs cost just four singles. Round about half past six bad light stopped play for the day and we had to return on the second day for about half an hour's cricket. Steele and Parsons were the overnight not out batsmen. There were eight overs to bowl and 41 runs required. Rice had the bowling organised so Hendrick could bowl half the overs. He entrusted Kevin Saxelby with the other four. Bruce French took a marvellous catch to remove Steele and I managed to run out Ken Higgs two balls later. This left the final pair at the wicket with nine deliveries remaining and 12 runs required. Hendrick finished off his over, conceding two singles. Saxelby now had to bowl the final over. Parsons hit him for four off the first ball. Two singles were run and four was needed off the final delivery. Parsons managed two. We scraped through to the semi-final.

By the time of the semi-final, Richard Hadlee had sufficiently recovered from his hamstring injury to return to the side. It was just as well. Without him we would have failed miserably. Lancashire decided to bat first, but never managed to raise their run rate much above three an over and only Maynard the wicketkeeper played with any freedom. He made 60 and Lancashire were all out in the 55th over for 182. Colin Croft then bowled at his most terrifying and quickly got rid of both Basher and Tim Robinson. By tea Clive Rice and myself had restored some measure of sanity and we were 63 for two. Clive was out in the 35th over and I was caught behind off Jack Simmons in the next over, so we were behind the run rate with only John Birch of the specialist batsmen left. Birch went eight runs later. It looked all up with us. Richard Hadlee however thought otherwise, hitting a six and half a dozen fours he took us into the Final.

This was the first time Notts had taken part in either the NatWest or Benson Final at Lord's and we went with great hope, even though the opposition comprised Somerset with their incredible trio of One dayers, Botham, Richards and Garner.

We were outplayed, outgunned and outmanoeuvred. Put in to

bat, the pattern of the game was a replica of the way Somerset had demolished Sussex in their semi-final. Paul Todd was bowled by Joel Garner in the third over; Robinson and I managed to see off the opening bowlers, but we both perished at 40. Tim pulled a short pitched ball into mid wicket's hands; I stepped back to cut Vic Marks and was bowled. Clive Rice hit out but after a beautiful six, was beaten by Marks and clean bowled attempting a similar shot. And so it went on. We were all out for 130 and Roebuck and Viv Richards knocked off the runs with no difficulty.

It was to be seven years before we came back to Lord's for a second Benson & Hedges Final. Half the 1982 side had gone. Richard Hadlee and Clive Rice had returned to their countries, except they still seemed to pop over to England pretty frequently. Basher Hassan was an umpire, Paul Todd had retired and John Birch was in charge of our Second Team.

Our first match was at Trent Bridge against Derbyshire. The Derbyshire attack, the main strength of which comprised Holding, Mortensen and Newman was as good as any, but they made the fatal mistake in this match of not having a fifth specialist bowler, but relying on one of the batsman who bowled to fill in. Mortensen, the Dane, needs very careful watching. In One Day cricket he keeps a careful line and makes the ball nip in or out. He continually mutters or chatters mainly to himself; fortunately for me I can't understand anything he says, so am not affected by him. He appeals more often than any other bowler in county cricket.

As a batsman he's not of much account, but I recall one match when he and the Scottish lad, Dallas Moir, were causing us problems. The wicket was fiery and we'd disposed of the main batsmen, but Mortensen and Moir used the ploy of putting their legs well down the wicket and despite their lack of batting talent we couldn't shift them. In the end Mortensen became fed up and ran about five yards down the wicket to Hadlee. Richard saw him coming and banged one in which just missed the side of Mortensen's head. I was at first slip: Mortensen is lucky to be still alive!

Franklyn is one of those batsmen who doesn't know what "steady" means.

Derbyshire made 178, which was a fair total for them. With our batting line-up we felt we would have few problems, but Holding and Mortensen thought differently. They dismissed Robinson, Newell and Johnson. Broad was run out—not by me. All of a sudden we were 36 for four. Franklyn Stephenson joined me at the wicket. Barnett, the Derbyshire captain, decided to keep the pressure on and bowled out his four bowlers—Base was the fourth. Holding did manage to clean bowl Franklyn, but I was still there and when Bruce French replaced Franklyn, Barnett had no resources left. He had to use his occasional bowlers. We hit 28 off three overs from Roberts and the match was won by a reasonable margin.

I was going to say that Stephenson is one of those batsmen who doesn't know what 'steady' means. He's a nought or fifty merchant, but in 1992 for Sussex he seems to be a changed man. Perhaps it's a passing phase.

The second match, at Oxton on Merseyside, was against the Minor Counties. It followed very much the pattern of the first.

We brought in Andy Pick for Kevin Saxelby, but otherwise fielded an unchanged side. One of the unfair things about the Benson & Hedges Cup is that three of the groups contain a weak side—Scotland, Minor Counties and Universities—whilst the fourth has only first-class counties. In this match, the Minor Counties decided to bat first, but only the captain, Plumb of Norfolk, managed to cope with our bowling and they were all out for 172.

Faced with this easy target we made rather a messy start. Broad, Robinson and Pollard were all out with just 55 on the board. I came in to partner Mick Newell. He was quite determined and stayed rooted to the spot whilst I scored most of the runs. He was in for the best part of two hours for 30, but played a valuable role. Eventually he was caught behind and Franklyn came in to knock off the rest of the runs. I received the Man of the Match Award.

In the third game, it was Chris Broad who held our batting together—the only two innings over twenty were his 53 and my 22. Yorkshire had put us in when play began an hour late. Bad light stopped Yorkshire's innings and we had to continue on the second day. Brian Clough turned up to support his native county and I remember his shouts of encouragement, but they did little good. Despite our total of 144 all out, Yorkshire never kept up the required run rate. Our fielding was top notch and Stephenson, Cooper and Hemmings all bowled very accurately. The way we played in this game proved that we had the spirit to turn things round and that we didn't get depressed when the match was going against us. Kevin had the splendid bowling figures of 9.5-3-9-4 and thoroughly deserved the Man of the Match Award.

We went into the final group game knowing that we had already qualified for the final knock out section. This fourth match was down at Taunton. Somerset had also qualified and all that remained was to decide which of us were drawn at home for the next round. Tim Robinson decided to bat on winning the toss. As with the Yorkshire match, our batting revolved around Chris Broad. He made 78 out of our 202 for nine. I didn't come in until 50 overs had gone and could do little more than hit out. Jimmy Cook the South African was in brilliant form. In something over two hours he hit 79 and by the time he was out—the score was 151 for three off 39 overs—we were clearly on our way to defeat. My friend Chris Tavare—the man who locked me out of my bedroom in Australia when I'd left the bath tap running—put the finishing touches to our fate.

We were drawn against Gloucestershire at Bristol for the Quarter Finals. Again Tim Robinson decided to bat first and again Chris Broad played a superb innings. The bowling was particularly strong. Walsh, Syd Lawrence and Graveney being difficult to make runs off at any pace, on the slow wicket which had been prepared. Everyone found it difficult to get the ball away. Broad scored 50 singles in his innings of 106 and my 21 comprised two fours and the rest in singles. We reached 134 for two at lunch, Broad was out at 209 for five and our total was 222.

Disaster hit us in the fifth over. Franklyn, bowling his fourth delivery broke down and limped off with a hamstring injury. Robinson put Broad on to finish off the over. Then Kevin Cooper continued in partnership with Andy Pick, who had opened with Stephenson. Stovold and Wright, who opened the batting for Gloucestershire found even greater difficulty than ourselves. The runs simply wouldn't come. At the end of the first hour, the total was only 30. I thought they were simply waiting to attack our fifth bowler (i.e. the replacement for Stephenson). Tim had the choice of himself, Broad, me, Newell, or Johnson. Chris Broad was the obvious choice, but owing to his long-standing injury he had not bowled for some years. Tim decided to try Broad. The batsmen ought to have attacked him from the word go, but he sent down little in-dobbers, which for some unknown reason the Gloucestershire batsmen treated with great caution. So Chris's 7.2 overs costs only 26 runs.

We were in complete control until Jack Russell came in at no.9. The score was 147 for seven. There were 11 overs left and it was growing gloomy—something after seven o'clock. Russell

Broad scored 50 singles in his innings of 106, his batting won the match.

went on to the offensive and quickly showed the specialist batsmen what they ought to have done. In three quarters of an hour he had hit 44 runs. Nine were required from the last over with two wickets in hand. Hemmings was the only main bowler who had not already completed the allotted 11 overs. Tim brought him back. Russell hit the first delivery hard and high. Broad took a good catch at long off. The batsmen had crossed and therefore Graveney, rather than no.11, Lawrence, faced the second ball. He nudged it for a single. The third ball, Eddie clean bowled Lawrence and we were through to the semis.

Kent were our opponents and they came to Trent Bridge. We were to be without Stephenson, but there were other changes and Kevin Saxelby, Andy Afford and Greg Mike all played.

We were put in to bat and the two left handers, Chris Broad and Paul Pollard gave us a brilliant start. The fifty was up in 12 overs and the hundred in 21. Pollard was out with the total on 141 and Broad did not survive long after that. I came in and was caught at the wicket off the first ball, from the medium pace stuff of Fleming. I could have kicked myself. I had my revenge on him the following summer. We went down to Tunbridge Wells. It was a glorious Saturday at the beginning of June. I batted just over three hours and scored 178; poor Fleming had 78 runs hit off his ten overs.

Returning to the Benson & Hedges Match, Greg Mike, the young colt brought in for the game, came to the crease on a hat-trick. He hit the second ball from Fleming for four and in the following over hit him for six. Our total was 296 for six off the 55 overs. Kent really hadn't much of a chance.

They didn't seem too cowed by the target. Hinks and Benson after a couple of overs to settle down got the measure of the two Kevins—Saxelby and Cooper. It was not until the third Kevin (Evans) was brought on that a wicket fell, Hinks being caught behind. The hundred came up after 21 overs, so Kent were keeping their run rate level with ours. The bowler who took the middle out of the batting and won the game for us was our left arm spinner Andy Afford. He captured four wickets in four overs for ten runs.

After that it was a formality and though Kent bravely kept the runs coming they eventually had no batsmen left—all out in the 49th over for 227—we were through to our second Benson & Hedges Final.

Essex were to be our opponents. They were regarded as the best One Day team in the country. We had a great deal to prove. After the retirement of Hadlee and Rice in 1987, our results the following year had been quite respectable in the first-class game, but very modest in all the One Day competitions. We had ended bottom of the Sunday League, with just three wins; the NatWest challenge had ended in tears in the Second Round; in the B&H we had failed in the Quarter Finals to the underdogs, Glamorgan. The cry that Notts were simply the two-man team of Hadlee and Rice had become shrill. Now came our chance to shut the critics up.

Our team was back to full strength. Paul Johnson, who had damaged his ankle just before the semi-final, was now recovered, as was Franklyn Stephenson. These two therefore replaced Greg Mike and Kevin Saxelby. Mum, Dad and Liz all came down to Lord's for the match. It was a glorious morning, the sun blazing down even before Gooch won the toss and decided to take first use of a perfect batting strip. The far-famed slower ball of Franklyn's dismissed Brian Hardie before he had scored, in the third over. This put us right on our toes. Graham Gooch was looking very permanent and the first hour produced 55 runs. Kevin Evans and Andy Afford replaced Coops and Franklyn. Andy clean bowled Gooch when he was 48 and the total 74. Mark Waugh, who had joined Essex at the start of the summer in place of Allan Border, arrived. He hit the ball very hard and in less than an hour had hit 41. Just on lunch Kevin Evans deceived him with a slower ball and so at the interval Essex were 156 for three. The game seemed to be going their way, but after lunch our bowling kept the runs in check. Alan Lilley, who a few years back had made a hundred on his debut against us, held one end and scored steadily, but no one stayed with him. Stephenson and Derek Pringle who were the two hitters in the side, were both run out. Stephenson and Lilley both found themselves in the same crease and Stephenson sacrificed himself. Even in the final overs, though they had wickets in hand, runs came in singles and leg byes. The total of 243 for seven was no more than we could have expected based on the quality of the wicket.

Our two left handers opened against the formidable Essex attack of John Lever and Neil Foster. Like Essex we soon lost our first wicket, Pollard being leg before to Lever, but more serious, a brilliant one handed diving catch off the same bowler, by Garnham, removed Chris Broad. Ten overs had been bowled and we were way behind the run rate, with just 17 on the board. Tim Robinson and Paul Johnson began the job of putting us back into the fight. To begin with it was slow work and when tea time came the score, off 25 overs, was 58 for two. This meant we had to score well over 6 an over for the rest of the innings. I wasn't paying much attention to who ate what for tea—I was too well aware that I was the next man in. When play restarted Robinson and Johnson got well on top of the lesser bowlers and there was a lot of talk about the absence of Acfield, who on paper was Essex's best spinner and who had been left out of the side.

The score rose to 149, when Foster, who had been brought back to stem the run flow, yorked Johnson. I came in and settled down. Only 13 had been added when I called Tim for a run. A rocket like return by Stephenson beat Tim to the crease and he was run out for 86. I felt sick. I didn't feel any better, when, next ball, Franklyn holed out to Gooch. That was the last ball of the 43rd over. We had 12 overs in which to make 82. Kevin Evans came to the wicket. We had no option but to hit out. In nine overs 59 runs came before Kevin was run out. I was not entirely to blame for that. 221 for six. I was caught by Mark Waugh on the square leg boundary off the fifth ball of the 54th over. We needed ten from seven deliveries. Having been responsible for running out Robinson, I came back to the dressing room, crept into a corner

Batting during the Benson and Hedges final.

Receiving our medals after the Benson and Hedges final.

and began packing away my gear. There was no way for anyone to score ten off the final over from John Lever. Someone shouted that we needed four off the last ball. I didn't want to watch. There was a yell from the balcony, "It's going." I looked up and saw the ball running away from Brian Hardie. Mum and Dad were seated in the stand with the ball coming towards them. Eddie Hemmings, who had struck the final blow was waving his bat wildly in the air. The Notts supporters in the ground exploded. I can't express the relief I felt: I hadn't thrown away the Trophy after all.

As a brief postcript, I had better comment on the return fixture. The Refuge Cup Final at Edgbaston right at the season's end. There had been prolonged rain early on the morning of the match and though the game began on time the outfield was wet and therefore the scoring was unlikely to be high. Robinson put Essex in and they scored 160 for five off their 40 overs. Apart from Paul Johnson, whose bat got entangled in his pads, all our batsmen established themselves and then got out—that includes me, clean bowled by John Childs. Ridiculous though it may seem and certainly it wouldn't be credible in a film, Eddie Hemmings was at the wicket when six runs were needed off the final three deliveries. He tried to hit Pringle for six and was caught by Mark Waugh at long on. We lost by five runs.

ESSEX v NOTTINGHAMSHIRE: Benson & Hedges Final

Played at Lord's, July, 15, 1989
Nottinghamshire won by three wickets.

ESSEX

1	*G.A. Gooch	b Afford	48
2	B.R. Hardie	b Stephenson	0
3	A.W. Lilley	not out	95
4	M.E. Waugh	c Robinson b Evans	41
5	P.J. Prichard	lbw b Cooper	1
6	J.P. Stephenson	run out	9
7	D.R. Pringle	run out	15
8	+M.A. Garnham	c Johnson b Evans	0
9	N.A. Foster	not out	2
10	G. Miller		
11	J.K. Lever		
	Extras	b 1, lb 26, w 4, nb 1	32
Total		(7 wkts, 55 overs)	243

1-4 2-74 3-156 4-162 5-185 6-220 7-235

Bowling	O	M	R	W
Stephenson	11	0	61	1
Cooper	11	3	30	1
Evans	11	0	28	2
Afford	11	0	50	1
Hemmings	11	0	47	0

NOTTINGHAMSHIRE

1	B.C. Broad	c Garnham b Lever	6
2	P.R. Pollard	lbw b Lever	2
3	*R.T. Robinson	run out	86
4	P. Johnson	b Foster	54
5	D.W. Randall	c Waugh b Pringle	49
6	F.D. Stephenson	c Gooch b Miller	0
7	K.P. Evans	run out	26
8	+B.N. French	not out	8
9	E.E. Hemmings	not out	6
10	K.E. Cooper		
11	J.A. Afford		
	Extras	b 1, lb 3, w 2, nb 1	7
Total		(7 wkts, 55 overs)	244

1-5 2-17 3-149 4-162 5-162 6-221 7-234

Bowling	O	M	R	W
Lever	11	2	43	2
Foster	11	1	40	1
Gooch	11	0	57	0
Pringle	11	1	38	1
Miller	9	0	50	1
Stephenson	2	0	12	0

Umpires: K.E. Palmer and D.R. Shepherd

Toss: Essex

Man of Match: R.T. Robinson.

CHAPTER 13

Results with a Difference

I think it's called a jinx—we have had, all in all, a terrible record in the NatWest Trophy, or Gillette as it was when I started playing. In each of the first three summers I was at Trent Bridge, we lost the only match we played. In 1971 and 1972 Hampshire sorted us out and in 1973 it was Middlesex. In 1974, for the first time, I was a member of a side which won a game—only one and that in the final over, against Warwickshire at Edgbaston.

By the time I'd completed ten years at Trent Bridge, we had won in those years, just five matches. Through the first seasons of the 1980s, our inability to win continued. We carried off the Championship in 1981, but we only crept through the First Round of the NatWest Trophy that year. In 1982 we reached the Benson & Hedges Final, but in the NatWest Competition we were taken to the cleaners by Gloucestershire in our second game; all out for 142—I was caught behind without a run to my name—Gloucestershire managed to score 145 for the loss of one batsman, a certain Chris Broad who hit 59.

And so, the sad run of defeats continued until 1985. Even then we nearly caused the biggest upset of all time in the very first round. Staffordshire came to Trent Bridge. Clive Rice won the toss and decided to bat. We blinked twice and two unknown medium pace bowlers, Maguire and Webster, had reduced the score to 71 for six. It was just after twelve o'clock. Bruce French went in to partner Paul Johnson. The unknown Webster bowled his quota of 12 overs straight off, taking the 6th wicket in his final over. We blamed the half past ten start for our mess and fortunately Paul and Bruce stayed together, added over a hundred and we finished with 243 for seven, Paul completed his hundred in the 59th over. Our bowling was clearly too good for Staffordshire and we kept their run rate so low that in the final stages even I bowled.

The second round match was also at Trent Bridge, against Warwickshire. We had the disadvantage of being without Clive Rice, who had had a finger broken whilst batting in the Championship game, immediately before the NatWest Second Round. In this match we were captained by Richard Hadlee—one of the few occasions on which he led the side. We were put in to bat and made another bad start, though not quite as grim as the previous game.

Tim Robinson retired with an injured finger off the second ball of the match. I came in and Broad and myself were getting nowhere. Off seven overs, we'd scored 15 runs. I thought, this is no good, and chanced my arm. I hit Hoffman for three successive fours, then missed the next ball and was bowled. Tim Robinson came back armed with a suitable bandage, when Broad's wicket fell, soon after my departure. Tim's an expert on pacing an innings in One Day Matches and the only mistake he made on that day was to finish two short of his hundred, though even then he hit eleven off the last over.

There was a curious coincidence at the start of the Warwickshire innings—I don't think, cancel that, I'm sure I've never seen it happen before or since. Off the second ball of the innings, Andy Lloyd retired hurt with a hand injury; hit by a ball from Richard Hadlee. Lloyd's injury proved much more serious than Tim's and he couldn't resume his innings. Dennis Amiss and Kallicharran batted well for Warwickshire and for the first half of their innings they kept up the required run rate. Then however they needed to accelerate but found you can't often do that against Kevin Cooper's bowling. At the other end Eddie Hemmings was out to prove how wrong Warwickshire had been to let him go. Kevin took four for 49, Eddie three for 27. We won by nearly a hundred runs.

We were drawn away to Gloucestershire at Bristol in the Quarter Final. Clive's finger had mended and we fielded our best side. The weather was lousy. We spent the first day watching the rain. We decided to bat when play started at ten thirty on the second morning. On paper Gloucestershire had a very formidable attack, Syd Lawrence, Courtney Walsh, the West Indian, Kevin Curran and David Graveney. On this occasion Lawrence and Walsh found it difficult to get their act together. Broad and Robinson put up the hundred at more than four runs an over. Graveney eventually broke up the partnership, having Broad caught. I made twelve in as many minutes, but was also out to Graveney. Robinson seemed sure to reach the hundred he had missed against Warwickshire, but ran himself out with 90 to his name. We had made 287 when the overs ran out.

The weather was now becoming pretty gloomy. Gloucestershire scratched about for 18 overs and made 42 without loss. The umpires then upheld an appeal against the light.

We took three early wickets next morning and seemed confident of victory, but their middle order, Brian Davison and Kevin Curran among them, hit out. In 14 overs the score leapt from 100 to 200. Fortunately wickets were falling, Richard Hadlee got Curran caught by French and Clive Rice ran out Payne, who was going well. When it came to the end 12 were needed off the last over, to be bowled by Kevin Saxelby. The last two batsmen were in, Jack Russell and Courtney Walsh. Russell hit a single off the first ball, but Walsh couldn't get anywhere and we won by ten runs.

The Semi-Final was yet another match which belonged to Tim Robinson, only this time he did reach three figures. The match took place at New Road, Worcester. If it hadn't been for the fact that we dropped Tim Curtis in the slips very early in his innings, Worcestershire would have been hard up to reach 150. As it was Curtis made 92 and they totalled 232 for eight. Our innings consisted entirely of Tim Robinson, I don't think I've seen him bat better than he did that day, or days—bad light stopped play early and the game spilled over into the second day. We were 137 for four, with Tim not out 75 at the start of that second day. Nearly a hundred wanted with only 14 overs remaining. It was a tough target. All I could do was sit and watch the morning's play. Broad, Rice and Johnson were the other three batsmen who didn't need to change. 64 of those final vital runs came from Tim's bat. Just as the end was in sight—we needed six runs—Bruce French hit out at Radford. A possible catch was dropped, but in the confusion, Robinson was run out. That left one over to go. Phil Newport was the bowler. I have always found Newport the most difficult of the recent Worcestershire bowlers—Radford has got me out more often, but probably because having concentrated hard combating Newport at one end, I have tended to relax my mind when facing Radford at the other. Anyway, I didn't envy Eddie Hemmings, the new batsman coming in to face Newport. The foolish Newport bowled a wide first ball; the second ball Eddie hit him for four and the third ball was a scampered leg bye: we'd won through to the Final for the first time.

Between the Semi-Final and the Final, Paul Johnson was sent off to hospital with appendicitis. The only selection problem we therefore had was who should take Johnson's place. Ken Taylor decided to play Duncan Martindale, the uncapped batsman who had appeared in several Championship games, but never played in the NatWest Competition. The story of the Final against Essex has been told before, but as, for the first time in the 1985 Competition I was going to make a worthwhile contribution, I feel I must relive that Saturday in September once again.

Essex were our opponents. They were without Neil Foster and played Ian Pont who had been on the staff at Trent Bridge for a year or two. It was a sunny day and the wicket was a beauty. Rice put Essex in. Richard Hadlee and Kevin Cooper kept the run rate down in the early stages, but Gooch and Hardie gradually established themselves. Gooch was dropped twice, Hardie mistimed a number of shots but no catches went to hand. They were still together at lunch and in the afternoon our confidence began to wilt as runs came with increasing frequency. Andy Pick did eventually bowl Gooch and Hardie was run out in a silly mix up, but Essex made 280 for two off their 60 overs.

Tim Robinson and Chris Broad opened our batting. Chris looked confident from the first ball. He was keen to catch the selectors' eyes and the plane to the West Indies. That's not to say Tim Robinson and I also had the same thought in our minds. As it turned out Tim went to the Caribbean and I went to Sri Lanka with the England 'A' side. It was a difficult decision for me. As it turned out it was not a very happy trip. The original plan was to go to Bangladesh, Zimbabwe and Sri Lanka, but both Bangladesh and Zimbabwe withdrew for political reasons—some of our players had played in South Africa. The tour ended up by being only to Sri Lanka. Most of the time we were stuck in Colombo, due to the battles with the Tamil guerrillas who seemed to control sections of the country. The weather was exceedingly hot and the object of the exercise was to blood young players for Test cricket. I can thank Derek Pringle for keeping me sane on that tour. He was educated at Cambridge, as was Edmonds, but unlike him, Derek seemed a normal, ordinary person. That came as a pleasant surprise.

Tim began his innings with a few streaky shots, but it wasn't long before the runs were flowing sweetly from both ends. By tea the score was 124 without loss. Twenty overs remained and the required run rate was just under seven an over. The first wicket to fall was Broad's. He attempted a second run, but was foiled by Ian Pont, who fancies himself as a baseball player, and whose throw came from the mid-wicket boundary. Fletcher adjusted the field for the incoming batsman, Clive Rice, and in the process upset

Batting against Worcestershire, Steve Rhodes keeps wicket.

Robinson's rhythm. His scoring slowed down and to compensate he hit Turner over the Tavern boundary for six, then attempted a second skier, which was caught by Brian Hardie. We were therefore 153 for two when I came in. Ten runs later Clive Rice was caught at mid-wicket, also off Turner. The light was beginning to fade. We needed 101 off the last 12 overs. Hadlee struck out in typical fashion, but his success, worth 22 runs, lasted only four overs, so that we still required 67 off eight overs. Rice had a difficult decision to make. The next batsman on the scorecard was Duncan Martindale—should Rice send him in, or try Hemmings or French? He sent in Martindale. We did nothing silly. No rash shots, no heart stopping dashes. It came to the final over bowled by Derek Pringle. He is not easy to score off. I was facing, Martindale had scored 20 and I had just reached 50. Fletcher set a legside field, but I managed to steer the ball to the off and by that method hit three fours and a two, plus another two between the mid wicket field. This left us with two to score off the final delivery. Again I tried to steer the ball away on the off side, but mistiming it sent a catch sailing to mid wicket. Essex had won by one run. That last shot was the difference between—in Bruce French terms—reaching the top of Mount Everest and tripping over just when you are about to plant the flag.

It was a sad day, but a week or so later, I was elected 'Championship Player of the Year'. I scored over 2,000 runs at an average of over 50.

I shall skip over 1986 and come to the NatWest Trophy Competition of 1987. In the first round we met Suffolk. These matches against the Minor Counties can be dangerous, but Suffolk had no well-known professionals in their side and it was to their great disadvantage to have to play at Trent Bridge. They decided to bat first, but Hadlee, Cooper and Rice were simply too good for the Suffolk batsmen. They were all out for 94 and we knocked off the runs for the loss of two wickets.

Our second round game was against Middlesex, but rather than play at Lord's, they decided to arrange the game for

Quiet and unassuming, Bruce often makes a useful contribution with the bat.

Uxbridge. We were asked to bat first. Chris Broad and Tim Robinson made an excellent start; 130 had been put on before a fine catch by Carr near the mid wicket boundary dismissed Robinson. We tried to keep the run rate flowing, but Middlesex possessed two wily spinners in Emburey and Edmonds, so whilst the score ticked on nicely, our batsmen were tricked into mistakes. John Emburey bowled me for 22. I'm usually happy against off spin, but I became too confident.

Middlesex had to face a target of 279. As Kevin Cooper wasn't playing, Hadlee opened the bowling with Kevin Saxelby. For once our strike bowlers failed. Wilf Slack, a brilliant player of fast bowling—I went to Sri Lanka with him and was amazed when I heard of his sudden death, he'd seemed so fit when on that tour—was not so keen on spin. Rice therefore brought Eddie Hemmings on after Hadlee and Saxelby had sent down four overs each. Sure enough in his second over, Slack went down the wicket to Eddie and, bingo, French stumped him. The pace of Andy Pick—he's much quicker than he looks—removed Carr. Gatting batted well. He'd come in first wicket down. The scoring rate fell and like us they lost wickets trying to speed up, but ran out of batsmen before they ran out of overs. We won by 60 runs.

The next two competitive matches were a Sunday League game against Warwickshire and a three day match with Leicestershire—we were now in mid-July. We won both and the first suggestions that we could go for the 'Triple', i.e. win the NatWest, the Sunday League and the Championship, were being made.

In the Sunday League game at Edgbaston, Warwickshire hit a good 175 and we were 70 for 3, both Robinson and Johnson out without scoring. I joined Chris Broad and together we added 109 for the fourth wicket, winning the game without losing another wicket. In the Championship match, Richard Hadlee dismissed Leicestershire for 174 and between showers we reached 58 for two by stumps on the first day. One of the two was Kevin Saxelby, sent in as nightwatchman, but quickly removed by

Agnew. I came in and watched as Tim Robinson batted out the final over of the day. In the morning we had been in about three quarters of an hour and were quietly building a partnership. We'd hit DeFreitas for one or two fours and he had a bit a stick from his mates. Suddenly from nowhere he produced a ball which jagged back and it hit me right on the end of the finger. There was a horrible crunch and I realised that something serious was up. I retired hurt. The finger was pronounced broken and that all but finished my season. I've been very lucky in that I have had few injuries and this one, in terms of matches missed was the most serious.

Mick Newell took my place in the side for the Quarter Final game at Derby and performed very well—he had actually scored 203 not out the previous week in the Championship match on the same ground and was thus full of confidence. His score in the NatWest fixture was 60 and the only other one of our men to reach fifty was Chris Broad, who made 67. Hadlee and Hemmings bowled with deadly accuracy and Derbyshire never looked likely winners.

The Semi-Final will always go down as Andy Pick's match. I travelled down with the team, but the finger was still mending and Newell held on to the place he'd earned against Derbyshire. The match was at Bristol. Gloucestershire were suffering from a clutch of injuries, several players turning out though not fully fit. There was nothing particularly interesting to note in the first half of the game. We scored 225, on a wicket giving some help to the bowlers. Pick opened the bowling with Hadlee and in the course of the first ten overs, Gloucestershire were simply destroyed. Their score was 23 for four. Pick had figures of five overs for ten runs and three wickets, Hadlee had conceded 15 runs and taken one wicket off his five overs. There was no way back and we won by 143 runs.

I hadn't been missed in those two games, but I feel I could have made a vital contribution to the Sunday League, which we were eventually to finish as runners-up.

We lost our last two matches in August. In the first of these, at Moreton-in-Marsh, against Gloucestershire, ten days or so after the NatWest semi-final, rain reduced play to 30 overs per side. It was a bowler's wicket and we dismissed Gloucester, having put them in, for 111. We reached 100 in the 29th over with a four by French off Walsh. French was out next ball. There were eight deliveries left, nine runs needed. Rice could send in Pick, Saxelby or Bore. He chose Pick. It was a baffling decision because Pick, at that time was liable to panic and have a wild swing at anything. Bore, in contrast, had proved his capability as a tailend batsman. My mind goes back to the famous Championship game against Somerset at Taunton, when victory would have given us the title. It had been in 1984. Rain had cut down the playing time, but Botham, captain of Somerset, had said to me that he would give us a chance. He was a man of his word. He declared and gave us 60 overs in which to make 297. Mike Bore went in at no.10 and faced the task of hitting 14 off the final over. He made 10 with two fours and a two, then was caught right on the boundary going for the winning stroke, off the fifth ball of that last over.

Returning to 1987, Hadlee scored a single off the first ball of the last over, Pick faced three balls without managing to score, then obtained a single off the fifth ball. This left Hadlee needing six to tie the scores. He hit a four.

That Sunday League defeat occurred on August 23; unfortunately we met with a second reverse at Derby the following Sunday. The fight for the Championship was also hotting up. In the Derbyshire three day game which surrounded the Sunday defeat, we managed a first innings lead thanks to a very attacking innings by Paul Johnson, but in the end the result depended on a sporting declaration and facing Mortensen and Malcolm we were unable to force a win. After the Derbyshire game, Sussex came to Trent Bridge, but I went down with the Seconds to Usk where we were playing Glamorgan. It was my first opportunity to try out my repaired finger. It was a low scoring game and I scored 50 and 15 out of Notts' totals of 181 and 130. The NatWest Final was scheduled for the day after the Glamorgan 2nd XI match.

I had been hoping to be fit for the Final and although unable to play in a serious match earlier, I had spent hours and hours building up the strength in my wrist. Ken Taylor asked if I felt I was fit to play—the choice he had to make was between myself and Mick Newell. Naturally I said 'Yes', but looking back on it, I feel the answer ought to have been, 'No'. It's one thing to play in a minor match and another to appear in a Final at Lord's. It was selfishness in my part and it was wrong. It could have cost Notts the match, because Mick Newell would have done a much better job.

The game itself turned out to be one of the most exciting I have seen—unfortunately very few people turned up to watch the vital finale. Rain messed up the Saturday of the game. Play started over an hour late. Clive won the toss and put Northants in. The match was officially reduced to 50 overs per side. Wayne Larkins and Geoff Cook opened the batting. Larkins bats very like Gooch. He is an outgoing character, completely opposite to his long time team mate, Peter Willey. Larkins however does not quite match the professionalism of Gooch. Geoff Cook was an ideal county player, but not up to international class. Cook and Larkins survived the initial attack of Richard Hadlee and Andy Pick, so that when lunch came Northants were 60 without loss—there'd only been an hour's cricket.

Second ball after lunch Bruce French caught Cook. We thought we had a breakthrough, but Lamb, after a few edgy shots, soon got the pace of the ball and runs were coming at about five an over. The clouds gathered, Larkins was trapped leg before; the rain descended. We took tea. There was a break of an hour. The sun returned, but it was obvious that the time lost would mean continuing on Monday. Bailey and Capel hit out and collected 45 valuable runs off the last five overs.

It was nearly six o'clock when we began our innings. The sun was so low in the sky that half the ground was in shadow and this

Hadlee and Hemmings leave the field after the famous victory at Lord's.

division between bright sun light and semi-darkness went straight across the middle of the pitch. Winston Davis opened the Northants bowling and in three overs he dismissed both Broad and Robinson. It was about the first time in the season that both our opening batsmen had failed. I came in first wicket down and Clive followed on at no.4. We saw off Davis and his partner Capel, but Nick Cook then came on and in his first over I tried to sweep and was bowled. My wrist still didn't react as fast as I was accustomed. Paul Johnson took my place and had not been in five minutes when he had his bat entangled in his pads and was leg before. At seven o'clock when stumps were drawn for the day we were 57 for four off 21 overs.

So with the match half finished we had to travel back to Trent Bridge for a Sunday League game against Essex. We were lucky that it poured with rain and no play was possible.

We had to travel back to London for the resumption of the game on Monday. It had been very wet and not until after lunch did play restart. I had no further part to play, and, having made a mess of my innings on Saturday, I kept a low profile. Clive and Richard were absolutely determined to win the game, although the odds were stacked against us. The required run rate was six an over. Rice and Birch, at the beginning, were happy to establish themselves. John Birch was bowled by Walker when he had made 21. Now the whole situation depended on Hadlee, the incoming batsman, and Rice. The required run rate climbed. Rice decided that he had to take risks. He reached 63 and the total 146 for five, when he lofted a ball from Williams straight to Geoff Cook at mid on.

Bruce French was our next man. Quiet and unassuming, he had scored some very useful runs in similar situations. He possesses the ability to become a fair county batsman, but that might affect his brilliance behind the wicket. The match was decided after French had been in two overs. Williams was bowling to Hadlee. Three times in that over Northants missed half chances—one fielder was blinded by the sun, the wicketkeeper

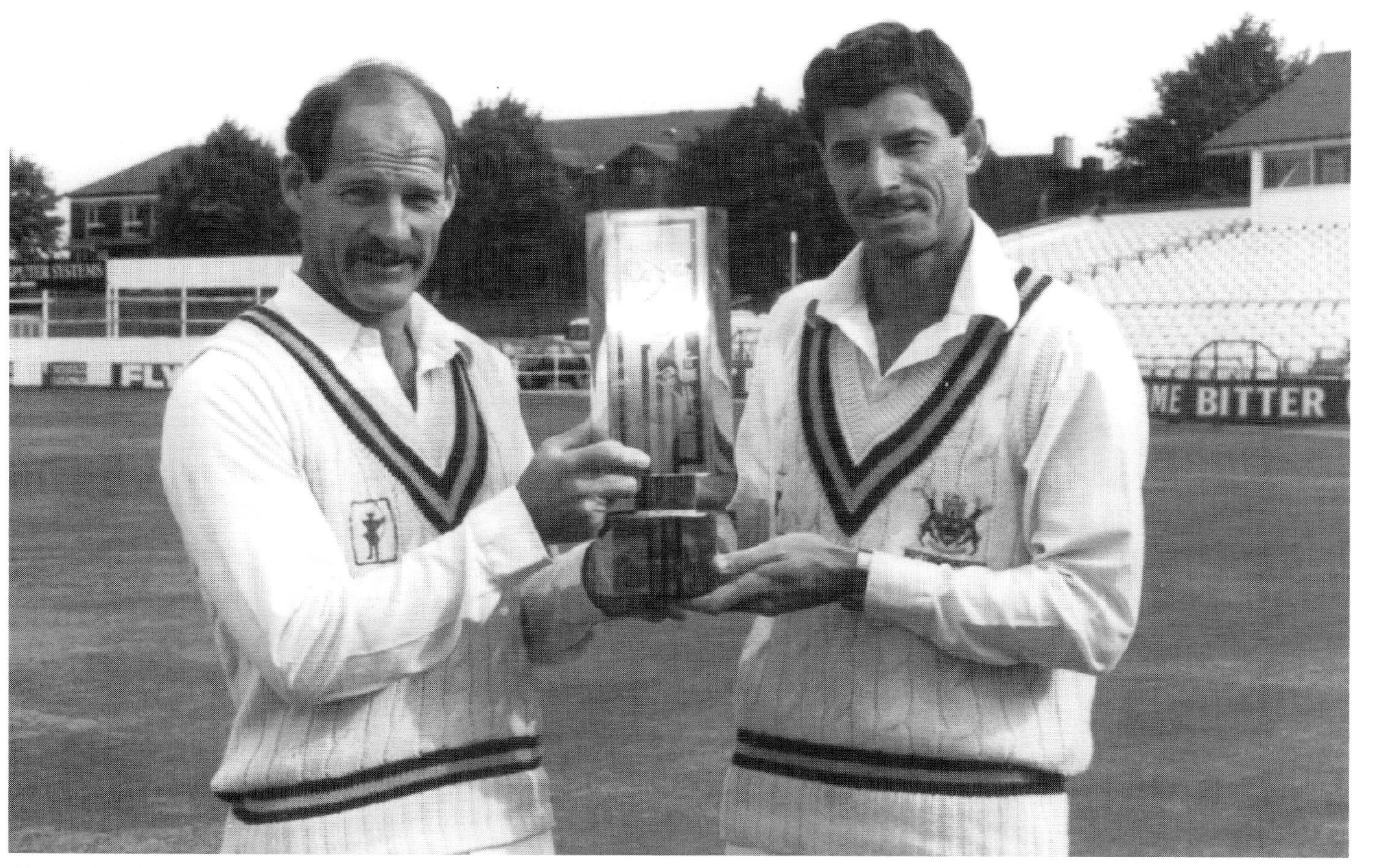

Clive and Richard bring the NatWest Trophy to Trent Bridge. They had inspired us to great heights.

Celebrating with balloons on the bus trip to the Council House.

fumbled a stumping and Allan Lamb dropped an ankle high catch. Fifteen runs came off the over. I could see the shoulders of the Northants' fielders droop. From then on both Hadlee and French played well and we actually won with three balls to spare, though French was run out quite accidentally at the start of the final over. So we won the NatWest Trophy for the first time.

The last match of the summer was the one which decided the County Championship, but only in retrospect. The fact was that the title rested between ourselves and Lancashire, but Lancashire's final fixture was a week after our own. Our last game was against Glamorgan at Trent Bridge. As had happened in 1981 we overwhelmed them. The difference between the Championship matches of 1981 and those of 1987 is that the wickets at Trent Bridge had come more and more to favour the bowlers. In 1981 a competent batsman could make runs at Nottingham, by 1987 it was, after the first day, much more of a lottery. The seam bowlers simply bowled a reasonable line and length and let the pitch do the rest. By 1992 the pendulum had swung back and gone beyond a fair wicket to one which more often helped the batsmen. The 25 point penalty had backfired.

Having beaten Glamorgan we sat and waited for the result of Lancashire's final match. Not only did Lancashire have to beat Essex, but they had to take maximum bonus points. Lancashire were put in to bat, could only gather two batting bonus points and the title was ours. So ended an incredible summer, at the close of which both Clive Rice and Richard Hadlee decided to retire from county cricket. They had inspired the rest of us to great heights.

NOTTINGHAMSHIRE v NORTHAMPTONSHIRE: NatWest Final

Played at Lord's, September, 5 and 7, 1987
Nottinghamshire won by three wickets.

NORTHAMPTONSHIRE			
1	*G. Cook	c French b Saxelby	26
2	W. Larkins	lbw b Pick	87
3	A.J. Lamb	b Rice	41
4	R.J. Bailey	not out	39
5	D.J. Capel	not out	29
6	R.G. Williams		
7	D.J. Wild		
8	+D. Ripley		
9	N.G.B. Cook		
10	W.W. Davis		
11	A. Walker		
	Extras	b 1, lb 2, nb 3	6
Total		(3 wkts, 50 overs)	228

1-61 2-152 3-169

Bowling	O	M	R	W
Hadlee	10	1	29	0
Pick	10	1	36	1
Rice	10	0	45	1
Saxelby	10	0	63	1
Hemmings	10	0	52	0

NOTTINGHAMSHIRE			
1	B.C Broad	lbw b Davis	3
2	R.T. Robinson	c Ripley b Davis	2
3	D.W. Randall	b N.G.B. Cook	10
4	*C.E.B. Rice	c G. Cook b Williams	63
5	P. Johnson	lbw b Walker	1
6	J.D. Birch	b Walker	21
7	R.J. Hadlee	not out	70
8	+B.N. French	run out	35
9	E.E. Hemmings	not out	0
10	R.A. Pick		
11	K. Saxelby		
	Extras	lb 18, w 8	26
Total		(7 wkts, 49.3 overs)	231

1-11 2-12 3-31 4-38 5-84 6-146 7-221

Bowling	O	M	R	W
Davis	10	1	45	2
Capel	6.3	1	31	0
Walker	10	0	38	2
N.G.B. Cook	10	2	30	1
Williams	10	0	48	1
Wild	3	0	21	0

Umpires: D.R. Shepherd and A.G.T. Whitehead

Toss: Nottinghamshire

Man of The Match: R.J. Hadlee.

CHAPTER 14

The Present and the Future

"How do you reckon I should finish the book, Dad?"

"You've got to explain what it's like knowing that in eighteen months time, the life you dreamt of as a schoolboy and then lived for well over twenty years is going to end. You've got to be serious and make a serious point."

"That's not Derek," chimed in Liz. "He can't be serious. Everything is a joke with Derek."

"It isn't, Elizabeth, it might seem like that, but underneath, he's serious. He cares desperately about cricket and Nottinghamshire cricket in particular. I know he acts on impulse and sometimes that can look like a couldn't-care-less attitude. That suicidal run the other day. He'd dashed off before his brains could tell his legs to stop. He was more upset than the batsman he ran out."

I listened to Liz and Dad debating me and how serious, or unserious I was. Mum and Dad had come to stay with us at Cropwell Butler for a few days. We were into the 1992 season. The book had to be finished. Time was running out. Liz had typed out my ramblings from the dictaphone and with the aid of Mum's scrapbooks adjusted things so they made some sense and ran in sequence. The sound of Megan practising her flute came from the

Chris Lewis came to Trent Bridge at the start of 1992. He is almost as sharp as Andy Pick with the comical retort.

dining room.

My foot was better. It had happened before—in New Zealand. Bernard Thomas had put extra padding under the instep. This time Sheila had sorted it out. We had reported back for pre-season training on April 1st as usual. There was a new face in the dressing room, Chris Lewis. He'd seemed quiet for the first few days, but once he adjusted to our way of going on he was almost as sharp as Andy Pick with the comical retort.

I suppose there always has been the conflict of dropping the old stagers in the team in order to give the youngsters on the staff an opportunity. I don't think it was quite the same when I started, because Notts were at a low ebb and the competition was more between the three or four young players as to which would fill a vacancy. In 1991 however we'd won the Sunday League and come fourth in the Championship. On paper we possessed a winning side and barring injury the only natural vacant spot would be when Chris Lewis was called up for England. In 1991 we had played an almost unchanged eleven all summer.

The conversation had moved on. Liz was explaining that Frances Edmonds wasn't as formidable and bossy in real life as she appeared on the telly. Dad asked me if he'd mentioned before that he'd played cricket on the Sydney Ground in Australia against Ceylon. Simon and his friend strolled in.

"I reckon they owe me an extra week's holiday, Grandad. I showed them how you taught me to calculate square roots: even the maths master didn't know how it was done!"

Megan had given up her flute practice and was in earnest discussion with her grandma. The book seemed to have disappeared from view. I wandered into the kitchen and decided on coffee. I took the typed pages of the book off the dresser. There was nothing mentioned about the last two or three seasons. The least said about 1990, for my point of view, the better. I'd had that niggling groin injury through most of the summer. The only game worth remembering was the three day fixture at Tunbridge Wells at the beginning of June. Broad and I batted 51 overs and scored

Catching Desmond Haynes in my last Lord's One Day International.

285. The rhododendrons of Tunbridge may cause hay fever, but on that Saturday the weather was great and all seemed well.

1990 was the final summer during which we were managed by Ken Taylor. I dare say I had caused him as many sleepless nights as any of the playing staff. I can't say I'd always agreed with everything he did, but looking at the other counties, I would suggest that the only other comparable figure is Les Ames of Kent. Ken had the respect of all us players. He didn't make decisions on the spur of the moment, but thought about everything he did in connection with the club. He would take me on one side, as he would all the other players, and talk through whatever problem or point he wished to make. He realised that I was emotional and impulsive and took that into account when deciding what to do with me next. It's vital that a club has someone like Ken. I felt that he was looking after my interests and the interests of the club in equal measure. Perhaps just as important he never acted from any selfish motive of his own.

When 1991 began therefore we were under the eye of John Birch, who had been the Second Eleven captain for the last two or three years. He had managed one or two soccer clubs and introduced a soccer-style training programme to our pre-season practice sessions. This was quite a controversial step. Cricketers seem to be divided between those in favour and those who prefer the more traditional net practices allied to the occasional jog.

Personally I don't feel that intensive fitness training is suited to cricket. Nearly all the other sports are of short concentrated bursts, such as 90 minutes of a soccer match, or most Olympic athletic sports, whether running, jumping or throwing. Cricket is six hours per day, six days a week for five solid months. That fact alone must put it in a different category. An hour's batting in the nets is worth any amount of physical jerks. Certainly the number of 'strains' that players suffer today is vastly increased on twenty years ago and one can't put that down to the increase in One Day Competitions because only the B&H Competition has been added during that time.

Before I launch into the season itself perhaps a few brief words on the players of 1991. Tim Robinson, the captain since 1988, is an honest hardworking cricketer who gives everything to the club. When he first turned up at Trent Bridge, he had long hair and a multi-coloured shirt. We thought this bloke will never make a cricketer, but now he is immaculate. His early batting had faults, he played too much on the leg side, but Clive Rice got hold of him and nowadays he plays very straight. He's a batsman to be relied upon, solid, dependable.

In contrast, Paul Johnson is a batsman to entertain the crowds. He's been on the staff for about ten years and only now is he becoming more consistent. He's one of the most exciting players to bat with. His weakness has always been impetuosity, almost the desire to hit every ball for four. However he is beginning to concentrate on building big scores and that's what is wanted if he is to break into Test cricket.

Mark Crawley who joined the staff in 1991 and is in his early twenties is a very talented straight player. He doesn't seem to have any obvious weaknesses against either spin or fast bowling. A shrewd thinker, he is a really good team man. What amazes me is his knowledge of cricket. He must have spent an enormous amount of time at Manchester Grammar School and then at University learning all he could of the ins and outs of the game.

The batsman who sees the ball earlier than anyone in our present side is Paul Pollard. He still has a bit of work to do against spin bowling and against balls outside the off-stump, but the same comment applies to all young players. He has the ability, the stamina, the will to do well, which combine to make him an England prospect. He likes to work hard and play hard. He has to be careful however, because to get to the very top you've got to dedicate yourself.

Chris Broad remains the best player of fast bowling in the country still. I think I related that story about him facing Malcolm Marshall earlier. Of the youngsters in the Second Team, Graeme Archer looks very promising and is a tremendous fielder, he

Paul Johnson is a batsman to entertain the crowds.

Andy Afford always enjoys a wicket.

reminds me of myself when I was a young lad. He can field equally well in the covers or close to the wicket and has a good eye for the ball. Mike Newell is a very reliable batsman, who is unlucky not to get into the side; it's the old, old story of only having eleven slots to fill. If Broad or Robinson were out of the side for some reason, Newell's the person to fill the gap and score runs for the side.

Kevin Evans is a player that people can easily under-rate. He's like Trevor Tunnicliffe, a very competitive type of cricketer. He's the best slip fielder we've got and in One Day cricket in particular he is valuable, especially as a bowler. The other all-rounder, on a par with Kevin Evans, is Mark Saxelby. It is a little too early to decide exactly how he will turn out, but he certainly has the talent. With the right encouragement and the right opportunities he could go far.

Andy Pick is a bundle of energy. He's always got something to say. In the dressing room the atmosphere can become very pressurised; Pick is the person who can break that down with a comment, not necessarily anything to do with cricket. He can bowl at the speed of light.

The other Andy, Andy Afford, has always had the ability to spin the ball, but with more chances in the First Team he is learning the rest of the craft of being a county standard slow bowler. Andy is not far off Eddie Hemmings' standard and to me Eddie's still the best spinner in the country. We've got Mike Field-Buss, but he's a more defensive type of bowler. One of our problems is that, with Eddie being so good, Mike Field-Buss has had very few outings with the First Team.

Bruce French is still as good a wicketkeeper as anyone in England. Day in, day out, he never drops a ball. He's become more outgoing in the last year or two and is a real driving force for the team. We'll find it very difficult to replace him, but he's still in his early 30s and should have at least another five years ahead of him. Jack Russell is probably the only keeper who is his equal.

Kevin Cooper, I hate batting against him in the nets; he

always gets me out with his late outswingers. He's been an underrated bowler all his career. He bowls on the spot all the time; if he lacks anything it's that little bit of extra pace—the nip that Mike Hendrick possessed.

One of the problems facing the county club in 1991 was finding the best partner to open the innings with Chris Broad. Paul Pollard had opened in some matches in 1990, but had lost his form, Mick Newell had also partnered Broad; Robinson had resumed his old position on a few occasions. Duncan Martindale and myself had also acted as openers. For 1991 it was decided that a new policy would be tried. I would open in the Sunday League games, but drop down to no.5 in Championship matches, when the opening slot would be taken by Paul Pollard. I know this idea had been tried by Worcestershire, when they decided to put Ian Botham in as Tim Curtis's partner, but they had not consistently used Botham as an opener to the extent that I opened in 1991. I suppose we were a bit lucky that the experiment worked straight off. In the first Sunday League game, against Lancashire at Old Trafford, Broad and I added 106 for the first wicket and the match was won by nine wickets. It was the first time Notts had ever won a Sunday League game in Manchester. When it came to the first Championship match, Paul Pollard opened and with Broad added 103 for the first wicket. A happy coincidence maybe, but these two partnerships set the scene for the summer.

In the second Sunday game, the first at Trent Bridge, we lost the toss and had therefore to face the formidable attack of Donald, Small, Munton and Reeve. It was the young England prospect, Tim Munton, who did the damage, removing both Chris Broad and Tim Robinson, very cheaply. Paul Johnson came in and together we began to rebuild the innings. With half the overs gone we only had 70 on the board. I fell to the off spinner Neil Smith at 75. Johnson hit out as did Franklyn Stephenson and we reached an unexpected 212 for six. It looked a reasonable total. Our bowlers soon made it a winning one. Eddie Hemmings showed what an attacking spinner can do—of course he is always that little bit keener against Warwickshire—and he ended with figures of 8-0-26-4. We won by no less than 82 runs.

We lost the toss in the third game down at Sophia Gardens, Cardiff. Alan Butcher decided to bat first and to prove his decision right hit up 77 off 83 deliveries. By some oddity of the fixtures we had played the Benson & Hedges Match on the same ground the day before, and Chris Broad had been out in the first over for a duck. When we started batting on the Sunday, Chris was quite determined not to repeat the unfortunate accident. By the time he was out we were 188 for four off 34 overs and he had made 108. We won with an over in hand.

Tim Robinson lost the toss yet again when Essex came to Trent Bridge for the fourth Sunday game; Gooch put us in. They were without Neil Foster. Our innings began with a stutter as Chris Broad was run out—was it my fault?—and again I fell to an off-spinner, this time our old Notts player, Peter Such. Our total of 194 for nine owed nearly everything to Paul Johnson's attacking innings. Considering Essex's powerful batting line up we didn't fancy our chances of success. At the start of the 38th over they needed only 14 to win with three wickets standing. Franklyn came on, replacing Kevin Cooper. He bowled Garnham with his first ball and Ilott with his second. Peter Such arrived to face a hat-trick and managed a single off the third ball. Singles were taken off the fourth and the fifth deliveries. With the final ball of the over, Franklyn trapped Topley leg before and against all odds we had won by ten runs with two overs to spare.

We had no problems sorting out Leicestershire at Grace Road—and Tim actually won the toss. Leicestershire began their innings in a rush. Mark Saxelby, Kevin's younger brother, put a stop to any run avalanche by taking four for 29 and we had a target of 171. The Australian Maguire dismissed Chris Broad and David Millns, the fast bowler from Clipstone, who had been on our staff, but got fed up, had Robinson caught behind. We were 34 for two. Paul Johnson and I added the best part of a hundred for the third wicket and I stayed on to hit Wilkinson for the winning four in the

37th over.

The Somerset game was much closer. We were put in to bat and I found it easy enough to score singles, but almost impossible to get the ball to the boundary—there were 31 singles in my 39. Even Johnno couldn't pierce the field and had 19 singles in his 31. Our total amounted to 180 for seven. We were fortunate that Stephenson managed to dismiss Jimmy Cook before he had his eye in. Only Harden of their batsmen came off, so their run rate was lower than ours and they had little hope of making 23 off the final two overs. With six matches gone we were the only county with an unbeaten record and it was beginning to seem that the Sunday League Trophy was in our sights. The next two games, against Somerset and Gloucester produced two more wins, but the rainy season had arrived. In the latter match, at Gloucester, rain chopped 20 minutes off the Gloucestershire innings and another 20 minutes off ours. When Middlesex came to Trent Bridge for the 8th match it was very wet and play didn't start until half past two. We lost the toss and Gatting, no doubt looking at the unsettled weather, put us in. Cowans had Broad caught off the first ball. The wicket helped the bowlers and although I stayed until the 24th over, wickets were falling at the other end. With Mike Gatting in command our total of 160 was never going to be enough and we went down to our first Sunday defeat of 1991.

We now had the first major alteration in our Sunday side—Kevin Cooper had been struggling to keep match fit despite a painful back and had been left out of the three-day matches. He now decided that an operation was necessary and therefore Andy Pick came into the side for the Surrey game at The Oval. Surrey had the new Pakistani fast bowler, Waqar Younis. He delivers the ball somewhat after the style of Andy Roberts and by the time of this match was carrying all before him in the Championship matches. We put Surrey in to bat; they put on 98 for the first wicket and were seemingly set for a very big score, but their middle batting failed and the target we faced was 186. The rain came yet again and our target was reduced to 162 off 35 overs. The damp ball no doubt hampered Waqar. Chris Broad and I virtually took the side to victory—I was bowled by Waqar with just eight runs wanted. We won with three overs unbowled.

The next two games both hinged on the final possible ball. In the first, against Hampshire at Trent Bridge, Kevin Evans hit four off the last delivery from Aqib Javed; in the second poor Bruce French was left with the impossible task of hitting six off the last ball—he was caught by Allan Lamb. That game of course was against Northants.

This loss made the Sunday competition more interesting: Lancashire overtook us at the top of the table, having a two point lead. We were without Mark Crawley for this game, Mick Newell coming in. This reduced us to five bowlers; more vitally we lacked Chris Broad—Broad's injury was not serious and he resumed his place in the next game, but Crawley had a broken thumb.

A win at Hove in the 12th game kept us just behind Lancashire—we were moving clear of the rest of the pack—but our next opponents were Worcestershire. The match had been chosen by Bruce French for his benefit game. The weather was glorious and a large crowd turned out. I've spoken about the bowling of Newport and Radford before; they were supported by Illingworth, the slow left arm bowler, who had made his England debut earlier in the summer and of course my old friend, Botham.

The mention of Botham always bring the story of the incident in Adelaide to mind. It's been printed before in a book or article, but the circumstances were not really explained and thus the whole point of the story really lost. In Australia we had been knocked out of the World Cup, quite unexpectedly by New Zealand. We were really down in the dumps. Like all these tours of the early 1980s England were playing Test matches around a Packer-style One Day Competition, so it wasn't as if we had been eliminated from the Cup and could now go home to lick our wounds. We had to pick up the pieces and carry on with the tour.

It was a red hot day, Botham suggested we went to a bar and

had a few drinks. After about an hour we had cheered up; some of us, including myself being more cheery than others. In walked a bird in a mini-skirt. Botham looks at me. There's not much difference between her height and mine.

"Bet you a fiver you can't change tackle with this bird."

I take on the bet, slip her a couple of quid and change into her skirt.

"Bet you another fiver you won't go out into the street dressed like that."

It was the main shopping street in Adelaide. I mince out in my mini-skirt and stand by the kerb. A car drew up and offered me a lift. I thought I'll go one up on Botham. I climbed in. The driver didn't seem to believe my garbled tale about being really an England cricketer. He thought it was some sort of come-on. I had to deal several blows with my handbag before being able to get out of the car and retreat back to the bar. The team had forgotten their worries and the cloud had lifted. Botham was always someone who could raise the spirits, even if we had one too many of them in the process.

We needed Ian Botham on the Notts side after this Worcester game. I hit fifty, Paul Pollard scored 73; our total after 40 overs was 209 for six. Tim Curtis, the Worcestershire captain, and Moody, the prolific Australian batsman opened their innings. Andy Pick had Moody caught behind in the first over. It was a great morale boost for us, but Hick arrived. If you remember he'd just been dropped by England following a series of low scores. Hick was out to prove the selectors wrong. I know the feeling too well! He took us apart, scoring 109 and being out with the score 188 for two. Luck was on our side, because Lancashire were also beaten the same day, therefore the gap between us and them remained just two points. There were three matches left: Kent, Yorkshire and Derbyshire.

We fielded very well in the Kent game and they battled their way to 137 for six off 30 overs. Their wicketkeeper, Marsh, and Ellison then hit out and more by good luck than judgement they

Batting with Tim Robinson in 1991 Sunday League

reached 217 for eight. Our innings followed much the same path though the scoring rate was somewhat higher, Paul Pollard attacked the bowling and like Marsh scored 56. We won with an over to spare.

Pollard had a lot to do with our victory in the next game at Scarborough, he hit another fifty in the run chase of the final innings, but was out and it was left to Kevin to score the nine runs needed off the 40th over. He did this by means of four twos and a single. An unusual ending.

So to our final match, which as it happened was against our next door neighbours, Derbyshire. We were now two points ahead of Lancashire. If we won the title would be ours; even if we lost Lancashire would have to win to overtake us. A record Sunday League crowd came to Trent Bridge to watch the game. The weather was warm, but cloudy at the start. We won the toss and put Derbyshire in. Our old campaigner, Eddie Hemmings, was missing, his place being taken by Mike Field-Buss; other than that we were at full strength.

Franklyn Stephenson had failed to agree terms for a new contract for 1992 and this would therefore be his last Sunday League game for Notts. He opened the bowling and in his spell of four overs did not concede a single run, at the same time dismissing Barnett, the Derbyshire captain. The only fireworks from the Derbyshire batsmen came from Azharuddin who hit a quick fifty, but they were only 176 for nine off the 40 overs. Devon Malcolm was unable to play, the major bowler we faced therefore was the Dane, Mortensen. He bowled well and I took care when facing him; for the rest the runs came easily. Chris Broad and I reached 134, before I was caught for 67 in the 30th over. After that Broad and Robinson coasted to the title. It was great to think that I had now been a member of the Notts side which had won all four of English cricket's major trophies, the Championship, the Benson & Hedges, the NatWest and now the Sunday League.

"Get a move on, Derek, where's the coffee?"

"Isn't it time Megan was in bed?" I countered. The best way to answer a question is to ask another, but Liz wasn't caught.

"She's been in bed half an hour at least."

I filled four cups and carried them through the dining room and into the living room.

"I forgot to tell you, Derek, I brought some photos of old Retford teams from Mrs. Brambrook. She will get them back, won't she?"

Dad got the photos out of a brown envelope. It was an odd collection. There were the Retford teams of about 1950 with the old pavilion behind them. That's what I was looking for, to give some idea of what the West Retford ground was like when I first knew it. Also there was the Retford Scorebook for 1927. A small pocket book with matches against such teams as Julien Cahn's XI, as well as the more familiar sides such as Creswell and Worksop. Some of the pre-war snaps had clearly been in someone's wallet for years and the corners were worn away and the pictures much creased. There was a short, tubby man in a Notts blazer and cap, cigarette in hand. 'Yours faithfully John Gunn' was signed across his trousers. The old folks in Retford used to talk about the time when John Gunn played for the Club. I doubt now if there are many who remember him actually playing. I shall have to go to the library and ask Peter if he can date the picture and how old John Gunn would have been at the time. It's not something we can put in the book.

"What's the next step with your book?"

"Liz'll have to sort it out. We'll have to get some statistics from Peter to put in the back and pick out the photos we want. I don't seem to be able to score a run this season. I made nought in the practice match, nought in the first Sunday game and nought again in the first Benson & Hedges game. A real record to put in the book, that is. I haven't the time. Give the typing to Albert Bocking or Les Bullimore. They'll help with the pictures."

We drank our coffee. Mum had some old black and white

film on the telly. I don't see much telly. One by one we drifted to bed. It was the Middlesex match tomorrow at Trent Bridge. I'd better score some runs. Someone said Phil Edmonds was going to play. Funny bloke, Edmonds.

Funny bloke, Edmonds.

A Statistical Summary

by Peter Wynne-Thomas

TEST RECORD
Series by Series

		M	I	NO	Runs	HS	Avge	100	50	ct
1976/77	v India	4	7	0	86	37	12.28	0	0	3
1976/77	v Australia	1	2	0	178	174	89.00	1	0	0
1977	v Australia	5	8	2	207	79	38.50	0	2	4
1977/78	v Pakistan	3	4	0	104	55	26.00	0	1	0
1977/78	v New Zealand	3	5	0	56	30	11.20	0	0	2
1978/79	v Australia	6	12	2	385	150	38.50	1	2	4
1979	v India	3	3	0	83	57	27.66	0	1	4
1979/80	v Australia	2	4	0	26	25	6.50	0	0	1
1982	v India	3	3	0	221	126	73.66	1	1	1
1982	v Pakistan	3	6	0	168	105	28.00	1	0	3
1982/83	v Australia	4	8	0	365	115	45.62	1	2	3
1983	v New Zealand	3	6	1	194	83	38.80	0	2	3
1983/84	v New Zealand	3	4	0	293	164	73.25	2	0	2
1983/84	v Pakistan	3	5	0	103	65	20.60	0	1	0
1984	v West Indies	1	2	0	1	1	0.50	0	0	1
Total		47	79	5	2470	174	33.37	7	12	31

ONE DAY INTERNATIONAL RECORD
Series by Series

		M	I	NO	Runs	HS	Avge	100	50	ct
1976	v West Indies	2	2	0	127	88	63.50	0	1	2
1977	v Australia	3	3	0	25	19	8.33	0	0	2
1977/78	v Pakistan	3	3	1	118	51	59.00	0	1	2
1978	v New Zealand	1	1	0	41	41	41.00	0	0	2
1978/79	v Australia	4	3	0	16	12	5.33	0	0	1
1979	World Cup	5	5	1	64	42	16.00	0	0	1
1979/80	B&H Cup	7	7	0	136	49	19.42	0	0	5
1982	v India	2	1	0	24	24	24.00	0	0	0
1982	v Pakistan	2	1	0	6	6	6.00	0	0	1
1982/83	B&H Cup	10	9	1	294	57	36.75	0	2	7
1982/83	v New Zealand	3	3	0	48	36	16.00	0	0	0
1983/84	v New Zealand	3	3	1	106	70	53.00	0	1	1
1983/84	v Pakistan	2	2	1	35	19	35.00	0	0	0
1984	v West Indies	1	1	0	8	8	8.00	0	0	1
1984/85	v Australia	1	1	0	19	19	19.00	0	0	0
Total		49	45	5	1067	88	26.67	0	5	25

NOTTINGHAMSHIRE

First Class Record Season by Season

	M	I	NO	Runs	HS	Avge	100	50	0	ct
1972	15	26	2	550	78	22.91	0	3	2	8
1973	19	35	1	906	107	26.64	1	6	6	9
1974	21	40	4	763	105	21.19	1	4	8	12
1975	20	34	5	1197	153*	41.27	2	7	2	7
1976	21	35	1	1540	204*	45.29	2	9	1	12
1977	13	23	1	401	63	18.22	0	2	3	7
1978	23	38	7	1461	157*	47.12	2	10	2	11
1979	11	22	1	1055	209	50.23	3	4	0	8
1980	22	37	1	1361	170	37.80	2	8	3	15
1981	18	29	5	1093	162*	45.54	3	6	4	21
1982	13	22	3	846	122	44.52	1	7	2	14
1983	15	22	1	583	94	27.76	0	4	1	17
1984	24	38	3	1527	136	43.62	3	12	3	25
1985	25	47	7	2151	117	53.77	5	14	4	24
1986	14	22	1	493	101*	23.47	1	1	1	14
1987	13	20	1	665	133	35.00	1	3	2	18
1988	21	37	4	1286	237	38.96	2	9	4	9
1989	24	41	6	1475	130	42.14	3	8	5	13
1990	15	28	1	987	178	36.55	2	5	4	14
1991	22	34	9	1567	143*	62.68	5	5	1	15
Total	369	630	64	21907	237	38.70	39	127	58	273

All First Class Matches

	M	I	NO	Runs	HS	Avge	100	50	0	ct
1972	15	26	2	550	78	22.91	0	3	2	8
1973	21	38	1	1013	107	27.37	1	6	6	10
1974	22	42	4	804	105	21.15	1	4	8	14
1975	20	34	5	1197	153*	41.27	2	7	2	7
1975/76 (SA)	2	4	1	58	43*	19.33	0	0	0	2
1976	22	37	1	1546	204*	42.94	2	9	1	14
1976/77 (Ind, Aus)	15	24	3	822	174	39.14	2	2	3	9
1977	19	33	3	709	79	23.63	0	6	4	12
1977/78 (Pak, NZ)	14	21	0	589	104	28.04	1	3	1	7
1978	24	40	7	1525	157*	46.21	2	11	2	11
1978/79 (Aus)	10	18	2	763	150	47.68	2	4	2	6
1979	14	25	1	1138	209	47.41	3	5	0	12
1979/80 (Aus)	6	10	0	250	97	25.00	0	1	3	3
1980	22	37	1	1361	170	37.80	2	8	3	15
1981	18	29	5	1093	162*	45.54	3	6	4	21
1982	20	33	4	1369	130*	47.20	4	8	4	18
1982/83 (Aus)	9	17	1	732	115	45.75	1	4	1	11
1983	18	28	2	777	94	29.88	0	6	1	20
1983/84 (NZ, Pak)	8	13	2	624	164	56.72	3	2	2	5

All First Class Matches (cont'd.)

	M	I	NO	Runs	HS	Avge	100	50	0	ct
1984	25	40	3	1528	136	41.29	3	12	4	26
1985	25	47	7	2151	117	53.77	5	14	4	24
1985/86 (SL)	5	8	1	212	92	30.28	0	2	2	5
1986	14	22	1	493	101*	23.47	1	1	1	14
1987	13	20	1	665	133	35.00	1	3	2	18
1988	21	37	4	1286	237	38.96	2	9	4	9
1989	25	43	6	1485	130	40.13	3	8	6	14
1990	15	28	1	987	178	36.56	2	5	4	14
1991	22	34	9	1567	143*	62.68	5	5	1	15
Total	464	788	78	27294	237	38.44	51	154	77	344

For Nottinghamshire Against Each Opponent

	M	I	NO	Runs	HS	Avge	100	50	0
Derbyshire	30	54	6	1862	237	38.79	2	12	5
Essex	15	27	2	981	117	39.24	1	9	3
Glamorgan	16	28	3	785	112*	31.40	1	5	2
Gloucestershire	13	20	2	674	85*	37.44	0	7	2
Hampshire	16	26	2	586	58	24.41	0	1	0
Kent	17	29	2	1144	178	42.37	2	5	1
Lancashire	31	50	6	1870	170	42.50	4	10	4
Leicestershire	34	62	8	2498	134	46.25	6	11	1
Middlesex	24	43	0	1603	209	37.27	4	9	5
Northamptonshire	16	23	1	510	84	23.18	0	3	3
Somerset	18	32	5	1054	204*	39.03	1	7	6
Surrey	18	29	1	844	106	30.14	2	4	7
Sussex	17	31	4	1059	157*	39.22	2	5	1
Warwickshire	23	37	5	1506	153*	47.06	4	9	0
Worcestershire	30	57	5	1948	122	37.46	3	13	6
Yorkshire	27	47	6	1541	166	37.58	2	9	5
Cambridge University	6	8	3	530	120	106.00	2	3	1
Oxford University	5	6	2	361	105	90.25	3	0	1
M.C.C.	1	2	1	84	52*	84.00	0	1	0
Australians	2	3	0	60	48	20.00	0	0	1
Indians	3	6	0	174	51	29.00	0	2	0
Pakistanis	3	4	0	43	38	10.75	0	0	2
Sri Lankans	1	2	0	66	52	33.00	0	1	0
West Indians	3	4	0	124	85	31.00	0	1	2
Total	369	630	64	21907	237	38.70	39	127	58

One Day Internationals

		Runs	Team Total	Catches	
Match no.1	England v West Indies (Lords's)		Aug 28, 29, 1976		Lost by 36 runs
6	c C.L. King b C.H. Lloyd.............	88	185	2	
Match no.2	England v West Indies (Edgbaston)		Aug 31, 1976		Lost by 50 runs
5	+c D.L. Murray b V.A. Holder........	39	173	0	
Match no.3	England v Australia (Old Trafford)		Jun 2, 1977		Won by 2 wickets
3	c R.B. McCosker b M.F. Malone....	19	173-8	1	
Match no.4	England v Australia (Edgbaston)		Jun 4, 1977		Won by 101 runs
3	+c R.W. Marsh b G.S. Chappell.......	0	171	0	
Match no.5	England v Australia (The Oval)		Jun 6, 1977		Lost by 2 wickets
3	c and b R.J. Bright......................	6	242	1	
Match no.6	England v Pakistan (Sahiwal)		Dec 23, 1977		Won by 3 wickets
4	+c Wasim Bari b Salim Altaf............	35	212-7	1	
Match no.7	England v Pakistan (Sialkot)		Dec 30, 1977		Won by 6 wickets
4	not out....................................	51	152-4	1	
Match no.8	England v Pakistan (Lahore)		Jan 13, 1978		Lost by 36 runs
3	c Mudassar Nazar b Wasim Raja.....	32	122	0	
Match no.9	England v New Zealand (Old Trafford)		Jul 17, 1978		Won by 126 runs
5	run out....................................	41	278-5	2	
Match no.10	England v Australia (Sydney)		Jan 13, 1979		Abandoned
	did not bat				
Match no.11	England v Australia (Melbourne)		Jan 24, 1979		Won by 7 wickets
3	c G.N. Yallop b G. Dymock..........	12	102-3	1	
Match no.12	England v Australia (Melbourne)		Feb 4, 1979		Lost by 4 wickets
3	lbw b G. Dymock.......................	4	212-6	0	
Match no.13	England v Australia (Melbourne)		Feb 8, 1979		Lost by 6 wickets
3	c K.J. Hughes b G. Dymock..........	0	94	0	
Match no.14	England v Australia (Lord's)		Jun 9, 1979		Won by 6 wickets
3	+c K.J. Wright b A.G. Hurst...........	1	160-4	0	
Match no.15	England v Canada (Old Trafford)		Jun 14, 1979		Won by 8 wickets
3	b R.G. Callender........................	5	46-2	0	
Match no.16	England v Pakistan (Headingley)		Jun 16, 1979		Won by 14 runs
3	+c Wasim Bari b Sikander Bakht.......	1	165-9	0	
Match no.17	England v New Zealand (Old Trafford)		Jun 20, 1979		Won by 9 runs
7	not out....................................	42	221-8	0	
Match no.18	England v West Indies (Lord's)		Jun 23, 1979		Lost by 92 runs
3	b C.E.H. Croft..........................	15	194	1	
Match no.19	England v West Indies (Sydney)		Nov 28, 1979		Won by 2 runs
1	c D.R. Parry b J. Garner...............	49	211-8	1	
Match no.20	England v Australia (Melbourne)		Dec 8, 1979		Won by 3 wickets
1	lbw b R.J. Bright........................	28	209-7	1	

A hook for four during the First Test at Perth.

One Day Internationals (cont'd.)

		Runs	Team Total	Catches	
Match no.21	England v Australia (Sydney)		Dec 11, 1979		Won by 72 runs
1	run out	42	264-7	1	
Match no.22	England v West Indies (Brisbane)		Dec 23, 1979		Lost by 9 wickets
1	c C.H. Lloyd b A.M.E. Roberts	0	217-8	0	
Match no.23	England v Australia (Sydney)		Dec 26, 1979		Won by 4 wickets
5	c G.S. Chappell b L.S. Pascoe	1	195-6	0	
Match no.24	England v Australia (Sydney)		Jan 14, 1980		Won by 2 wickets
6	c L.S. Pascoe b G.S. Chappell	0	164-8	2	
Match no.25	England v West Indies (Adelaide)		Jan 16, 1980		Lost by 107 runs
6	b A.M.E. Roberts	16	139	0	
Match no.26	England v India (Headingley)		Jun 2, 1982		Won by 9 wickets
	did not bat		194-1	0	
Match no.27	England v India (The Oval)		Jun 4, 1982		Won by 114 runs
6	run out	24	276-9	0	
Match no.28	England v Pakistan (Trent Bridge)		Jul 17, 1982		Won by 7 wickets
	did not bat		252-3	0	
Match no.29	England v Pakistan (Old Trafford)		Jul 19, 1982		Won by 73 runs
6	run out	6	295-8	1	
Match no.30	England v Australia (Sydney)		Jan 11, 1983		Lost by 31 runs
4	b C.G. Rackemann	5	149	1	
Match no.31	England v New Zealand (Melbourne)		Jan 13, 1983		Lost by 2 runs
6	c M.C. Snedden b J.V. Coney	8	237-8	2	
Match no.32	England v New Zealand (Brisbane)		Jan 15, 1983		Won by 54 runs
6	run out	34	267-6	1	
Match no.33	England v Australia (Brisbane)		Jan 16, 1983		Lost by 7 wickets
6	b G.F. Lawson	57	182	0	
Match no.34	England v New Zealand (Sydney)		Jan 20, 1983		Won by 8 wickets
	did not bat		202-2	1	
Match no.35	England v Australia (Melbourne)		Jan 23, 1983		Lost by 5 wickets
5	not out	51	213-5	0	
Match no.36	England v Australia (Sydney)		Jan 26, 1983		Won by 98 runs
5	run out	47	207	1	
Match no.37	England v New Zealand (Adelaide)		Jan 29, 1983		Lost by 4 wickets
4	c J.G. Wright b M.C. Snedden	31	296-5	0	
Match no.38	England v Australia (Adelaide)		Jan 30, 1983		Won by 14 runs
5	c and b G.F. Lawson	49	228-6	1	
Match no.39	England v New Zealand (Perth)		Feb 5, 1983		Lost by 7 wickets
5	c G.P. Howarth b M.C. Snedden	12	88-7	0	
Match no.40	England v New Zealand (Auckland)		Feb 19, 1983		Lost by 6 wickets
5	b E.J. Chatfield	30	184-9	0	

Running out Rick McCosker at Headingley.

One Day Internationals (cont'd.)

		Runs	Team Total	Catches	
Match no.41	England v New Zealand (Wellington)		Feb 23, 1983		Lost by 103 runs
5	c G.P. Howarth b J.F.W. Morrison..	16	192	0	
Match no.42	England v New Zealand (Christchurch)		Feb 26, 1983		Lost by 84 runs
6	b J.V. Coney............................	2	127	0	
Match no.43	England v New Zealand (Christchurch)		Feb 18, 1984		Won by 54 runs
4	c B.L. Cairns b R.J. Hadlee..........	70	188-9	0	
Match no.44	England v New Zealand (Wellington)		Feb 22, 1984		Won by 6 wickets
4	not out..................................	25	139-4	1	
Match no.45	England v New Zealand (Auckland)		Feb 25, 1984		Lost by 7 wickets
4	b S.L. Boock............................	11	209-9	0	
Match no.46	England v Pakistan (Lahore)		Mar 9, 1984		Lost by 6 wickets
5	run out..................................	16	184-8	0	
Match no.47	England v Pakistan (Karachi)		Mar 26, 1984		Won by 6 wickets
6	not out..................................	19	164-4	0	
Match no.48	England v West Indies (Lord's)		Jun 4, 1984		Lost by 8 wickets
6	+c P.J. Dujon b M.D. Marshall.......	8	196-9	1	
Match no.49	England v Australia (Sharjah)		Mar 24, 1985		Lost by 2 wickets
4	+st S.J. Rixon b M.J. Bennett..........	19	177-8	0	

Note:

The number before each batting line denotes the position in which Randall batted.
+ before the fielder's name denotes that he kept wicket.

Career Test Scores

		Runs	Team Total	Catches	
1976/77					
Match no.1	England v India (Calcutta)		Jan 1, 2, 4, 5, 6		Won by
4	lbw b E.A.S. Prasanna.................	37	321	0	10 wickets
	did not bat		16-0		
Match no.2	England v India (Madras)		Jan 14, 15, 16, 18, 19		Won by 200 runs
4	run out....................................	2	262	1	
5	+c S.M.H. Kirmani b B.S. Chandrasekhar	0	185-9d	0	
Match no.3	England v India (Bangalore)		Jan 28, 29, 30, Feb 1, 2		Lost by 140 runs
4	c Yajuvendra b E.A.S. Prasanna.....	10	195	1	
4	c A.D. Gaekwad b B.S. Bedi..........	0	177	1	
Match no.4	England v India (Bombay)		Feb 11, 12, 14, 15, 16		Drawn
3	c A.D. Gaekwad b E.A.S. Prasanna.	22	317	0	
3	+c S.M.H. Kirmani b K.D. Ghavri....	15	152-7	0	
Match no.5	England v Australia (Melbourne)		Mar 12, 13, 14, 16, 17		Lost by 45 runs
4	+c R.W. Marsh b D.K. Lillee..........	4	95	0	
4	c G.J. Cosier b K.J. O'Keeffe.........	174	417	0	
1977					
Match no.6	England v Australia (Lord's)		Jun 16, 17, 18, 20, 21		Drawn
4	c G.S. Chappell b M.H.N. Walker...	53	216	0	
7	c R.B. McCosker b J.R. Thomson...	0	305	0	
Match no.7	England v Australia (Old Trafford)		Jul 7, 8, 9, 11, 12		Won by 9 wickets
4	lbw b R.J. Bright.........................	79	437	0	
	did not bat		82-1	2	
Match no.8	England v Australia (Trent Bridge)		Jul 28, 29, 30, Aug 1, 2		Won by 7 wickets
4	run out....................................	13	364	0	
5	not out....................................	19	189-3	1	
Match no.9	England v Australia (Headingley)		Aug 11, 12, 13, 15		Won by inns
4	lbw b L.S. Pascoe.......................	20	436	1	and 85 runs
				(2nd inns)	
Match no.10	England v Australia (The Oval)		Aug 25, 26, 27, 29, 30		Drawn
4	+c R.W. Marsh b M.F. Malone........	3	214	0	
4	not out....................................	20	57-2		
1977/78					
Match no.11	England v Pakistan (Lahore)		Dec 14, 15, 16, 18, 19		Drawn
4	c Iqbal Qasim b Liaqat Ali.............	19	288	0	
	did not bat			0	1-0-2-0
Match no.12	England v Pakistan (Hyderabad)		Jan 2, 3, 4, 6, 7		Drawn
4	c and b Abdul Qadir....................	7	191	0	
	did not bat		186-1	0	

Career Test Scores (cont'd.)

		Runs	Team Total	Catches	
1977/78 (cont'd.)					
Match no.13	England v Pakistan (Karachi)		Jan 18, 19, 20, 22, 23		Drawn
3	lbw b Iqbal Qasi	23	266	0	
3	b Sikander Bakht	55	222-5		
Match no.14	England v New Zealand (Wellington)		Feb 10, 11, 12, 14, 15		Lost by 72 runs
5	c M.G. Burgess b R.J. Hadlee	4	215	0	
4	lbw b R.O. Collinge	9	64	0	
Match no.15	England v New Zealand (Christchurch)		Feb 24, 25, 26, 28, Mar 1		Won by 174 runs
3	c M.G. Burgess b R.J. Hadlee	0	418	0	
3	run out	13	96-4d	0	
Match no.16	England v New Zealand (Auckland)		Mar 4, 5, 6, 8, 9, 10		Drawn
2	lbw b R.J. Hadlee	30	429	1	
	did not bat			1	1-0-1-0
1978/79					
Match no.17	England v Australia (Brisbane)		Dec 1, 2, 3, 5, 6		Won by 7 wickets
3	c T.J. Laughlin b A.G. Hurst	75	286	0	
3	not out	74	170-3	0	
Match no.18	England v Australia (Perth)		Dec 15, 16, 17, 19, 20		Won by 166 runs
3	c G.M. Wood b R.M. Hogg	0	309	0	
3	c G.J. Cosier b B. Yardley	45	208	0	
Match no.19	England v Australia (Melbourne)		Dec 29, 30, Jan 1, 2, 3		Lost by 103 runs
3	lbw b A.G. Hurst	13	143	2	
3	lbw b R.M. Hogg	2	179	1	
Match no.20	England v Australia (Sydney)		Jan 6, 7, 8, 10, 11		Won by 93 runs
3	c G.M. Wood b A.G. Hurst	0	152	0	
3	lbw b R.M. Hogg	150	346	0	
Match no.21	England v Australia (Adelaide)		Jan 27, 28, 29, 31, Feb 1		Won by 205 runs
3	c P.H. Carlson b A.G. Hurst	4	169	1	
3	c B. Yardley b A.G. Hurst	15	360	0	
Match no.22	England v Australia (Sydney)		Feb 10, 11, 12, 14		Won by 9 wickets
3	lbw b R.M. Hogg	7	308	0	
3	not out	0	35-1	0	
1979					
Match no.23	England v India (Edgbaston)		Jul 12, 13, 14, 16		Won by inns
3	+c B. Reddy b Kapil Dev	15	633-5d	0	and 83 runs
	did not bat			2	
Match no.24	England v India (Lord's)		Aug 2, 3, 4, 6, 7		Drawn
5	run out	57	419-9d	1	
	did not bat			1	

Career Test Scores (cont'd.)

		Runs	Team Total	Catches	
1979 (cont'd.)					
Match no.25	England v India (Headingley)		Aug 16, 17, 18, 20, 21		Drawn
5	b K.D. Ghavri	11	270	0	
1979/80					
Match no.26	England v Australia (Perth)		Dec 14, 15, 16, 18, 19		Lost by 138 runs
1	c K.J. Hughes b D.K. Lillee	0	228	0	
1	lbw b G. Dymock	1	215	1	
Match no.27	England v Australia (Sydney)		Jan 4, 5, 6, 8		Lost by 6 wickets
3	c G.S. Chappell b D.K. Lillee	0	123	0	
6	+c R.W. Marsh b G.S. Chappell	25	237	0	
1982					
Match no.28	England v India (Lord's)		Jun 10, 11, 12, 14, 15		Won by 7 wickets
6	c G.A. Parker b Kapil Dev	126	433	0	
	did not bat		67-3		
Match no.29	England v India (Old Trafford)		Jun 24, 25, 26, 27, 28		Drawn
6	+c S.M.H. Kirmani b D.R. Doshi	0	425	1	
Match no.30	England v India (The Oval)		Jul 8, 9, 10, 12, 13		Drawn
6	+st S.M.H. Kirmani b R.J. Shastri	95	594	0	
	did not bat		191-3d		
Match no.31	England v Pakistan (Edgbaston)		Jul 29, 30, 31, August 1		Won by 113 runs
1	b Imran Khan	17	272	0	
1	b Imran Khan	105	291	1	
Match no.32	England v Pakistan (Lord's)		Aug 12, 13, 14, 15, 16		Lost by 10 wickets
1	b Sarfraz Nawaz	29	227	0	
1	b Mudassar Nazar	9	276	0	
Match no.33	England v Pakistan (Headingley)		Aug 26, 27, 28, 30, 31		Won by 3 wickets
7	run out	8	256	0	
7	lbw b Imran Khan	0	219-7	2	
1982/83					
Match no.34	England v Australia (Perth)		Nov 12, 13, 14, 16, 17		Drawn
6	c G.M. Wood b B. Yardley	78	411	0	
6	b G.F. Lawson	115	358	0	
Match no.35	England v Australia (Brisbane)		Nov 26, 27, 28, 30, Dec 1		Lost by 7 wickets
6	c G.F. Lawson b C.G. Rackemann	37	219	1	
5	c B. Yardley b J.R. Thomson	4	309	0	
Match no.36	England v Australia (Brisbane)		Dec 10, 11, 12, 14, 15		Lost by 8 wickets
6	b G.F. Lawson	0	216	0	
6	+c R.W. Marsh b G.F. Lawson	17	304	1	

Career Test Scores (cont'd.)

		Runs	Team Total	Catches	
1982/83 (cont'd.)					
Match no.37	England v Australia (Sydney)		Jan 2, 3, 4, 6, 7		Drawn
5	b J.R. Thomson	70	237	0	
6	b J.R. Thomson	44	314-7	1	
1983					
Match no.38	England v New Zealand (The Oval)		Jul 14, 15, 16, 17, 18		Won by 189 runs
6	not out	75	209	1	
6	c J.V. Coney b R.J. Hadlee	3	446-6d	0	
Match no.39	England v New Zealand (Headingley)		Jul 28, 29, 30, Aug 1		Lost by 5 wickets
6	c J.V. Coney b B.L. Cairns	4	225	0	
6	+c I.D.S. Smith b E.J. Chatfield	16	252	2	
Match no.40	England v New Zealand (Trent Bridge)		Aug 25, 26, 27, 28, 29		Won by 165 runs
7	c B.A. Edgar b R.J. Hadlee	83	420	0	
7	b R.J. Hadlee	13	297	0	
1983/84					
Match no.41	England v New Zealand (Wellington)		Jan 20, 21, 22, 23, 24		Drawn
7	c M.D. Crowe b R.J. Hadlee	164	463	0	
	did not bat		69-0		
Match no.42	England v New Zealand (Christchurch)		Feb 3, 4, 5		Lost by inns
5	c J.V. Coney b R.J. Hadlee	0	82	1	and 132 runs
7	c B.L. Cairns b R.J. Hadlee	25	93		
Match no.43	England v New Zealand (Auckland)		Feb 10, 11, 12, 14, 15		Drawn
5	c J.G. Wright b E.J. Chatfield	104	439	1	
Match no.44	England v Pakistan (Karachi)		Mar 2, 3, 4, 6		Lost by 3 wickets
5	b Abdul Qadir	8	182	0	
5	b Abdul Qadir	16	159	0	
Match no.45	England v Pakistan (Faisalabad)		Mar 12, 13, 14, 16, 17		Drawn
3	b Sarfraz Nawaz	65	546-8d	0	
Match no.46	England v Pakistan (Lahore)		Mar 19, 20, 21, 23, 24		Drawn
5	c Salim Malik b Abdul Qadir	14	241	0	
6	c Salim Malik b Abdul Qadir	0	344-9d	0	
1984					
Match no.47	England v West Indies (Edgbaston)		Jun 14, 15, 16, 18		Lost by inns
3	b J. Garner	0	191	1	and 180 runs
3	c C.H. Lloyd b J. Garner	1	235		

Running out Gordon Greenidge in the World Cup.

And he's out.

D.W. RANDALL: How he was out, Season by Season 1972 to 1991

	72	73	74	75	75/6	76	76/7	77	77/8	78	78/9	79	79/80	80	81	82	82/3	83	83/4	84	85	85/6	86	87	88	89	90	91	Total
Bowled	3	5	8	3	1	9	1	2	4	9	2	3	0	5	2	10	6	7	3	7	10	0	6	3	8	7	4	6	134
Caught	15	18	20	20	1	22	14	15	10	21	10	16	9	20	15	12	10	14	8	25	27	4	11	12	19	20	17	15	420
LBW	5	11	7	3	1	2	4	11	6	2	4	2	1	10	4	4	0	5	0	2	2	2	3	4	4	9	5	3	116
Run Out	0	2	1	2	0	2	2	2	1	0	0	2	0	0	2	2	0	0	0	2	1	0	1	0	2	0	1	1	26
Stumped	1	1	2	1	0	1	0	0	0	1	0	1	0	1	1	1	0	0	0	1	0	1	0	0	0	1	0	0	14
Total	24	37	38	29	3	36	21	30	21	33	16	24	10	36	24	29	16	26	11	37	40	7	21	19	33	37	27	25	710

How Randall Was Out in Comparison with other Batsmen

	Randall	Ranji	Donnelly	Woolley	Tarrant	Armstrong	Merchant	Headley
Bowled	19%	27%	19%	28%	22%	45%	22%	10%
Caught	59%	57%	52%	54%	61%	38%	48%	43%
LBW	16%	8%	15%	12%	10%	8%	22%	19%
Run Out	4%	4%	1%	3%	4%	4%	6%	5%
Stumped	2%	5%	8%	3%	3%	5%	2%	5%

The Bowlers Responsible

11 times dismissed by: R.J. Hadlee
10 times dismissed by: N.V. Radford
9 times dismissed by: Imran Khan
8 times dismissed by: W.W. Daniel and J.E. Emburey
7 times dismissed by: P.B. Clift and N. Gifford
6 times dismissed by: J. Birkenshaw, Abdul Qadir, S.T. Clarke, P.H. Edmonds, N.M. McVicker, P. Lever, C.M. Old, P.I. Pocock, G. Miller, J.F. Steele, A. Sidebottom
5 times dismissed by: K.D. Boyce, J.P. Agnew, P. Carrick, J.D. Inchmore, A.G. Hurst, M.D. Marshall, N.A. Foster, H.R. Moseley, A.P. Pridgeon, O.H. Mortensen, D.L. Underwood, L.B. Taylor, C.E. Waller, J.R. Thomson, M. Watkinson
4 times dismissed by: G.A. Cope, B.S. Bedi, W.K.M. Benjamin, R.M. Hogg, M. Hendrick, I. Folley, S.P. Hughes, V.J. Marks, M.J. Holding, D.K, Lillee, N.A. Mallender, S. Venkataraghavan, C.J. Tunnicliffe, Sarfraz Nawaz, G.C. Small, N.F. Williams